An Orality Primer for Missionaries

Daniel Sheard
dssheard@wanadoo.fr

An Orality Primer for Missionaries

Printed and bound in the United States of America
First Edition
ISBN 978-0-9801153-0-7
Orders: dssheard@wanadoo.fr

This book is available in special quantity discounts when purchased in bulk for organizations, mission agencies, schools, seminaries, churches, and special interest groups. For information, please contact the author using the email address above.

To Sue,

A virtuous woman, who can find?

. . . which things also we

speak

not in the words

which man's wisdom teaches,

but which the Spirit teaches,

combining spiritual ideas

with spiritual words.

1 Corinthians 2:13

Contrasts

Painting Two Pictures

Imagine for a minute, your typical adult home Bible study in the United States. People drive up to a home, get out of their cars, ring the doorbell, and walk into a living room where there is a circle of chairs. A person brings a guitar and song books.

"Let's get started," the leader says.

"Everyone take this songbook and open to song #33, *Here I am to Worship*. Jim brought his guitar tonight. We'll sing some before we get started with our Bible Study."

After some singing, prayer, and chat, the leader instructs everyone to take their Bible and their Bible study book and starts asking questions.

"How did everyone make out this week finishing the chapters? Did you get a chance to do them? We'll start with Chapter Three and discuss the questions on page 47. Our text for tonight is Acts 13 concerning the call of Paul to the mission field. Sue, would you read Acts 13, verses 1-4, after everyone has found the passage?"

The evening continues pretty much like this for the next hour, reading and discussing, reading and discussing.

What would happen to this same scenario in an oral culture? First, you likely would not be in a home. They are too poor to have 12 chairs. You may be under a tree, in a public place in a village, or, if you are in a home, most people are likely sitting on the floor.

The members of the Bible study did not drive to the house. They either walked or took public transport.

They would walk into the gathering without a Bible. They don't know how to read. If they do show up with a Bible, don't call on them to read, because they don't read well enough to make it through a verse. They are terrified that you might call on them. They carry their Bible out of respect and love for God.

They are all sitting there chatting. The leader says, "Let's get started."

Stop! What do you think happens next? They have no song books, no Bibles, and nothing on their laps. All they have are their ears and mouth. How would you teach them? What would you teach them? Will you sing? How will you fill one hour of discipleship time?

Even more than that, when they leave, will they know the Word of God better? How will you know they do?

When they return next week, what did you ask them to do during the week to reinforce what you told them? They have no Bible to consult, to read, or to help them maintain their spiritual life.

What will you expect of them? Are you uncertain if you as the teacher will even make it through the hour? How will they ever achieve spiritual maturity? How will they master what they hear?

Contents

Preface
The Road Less Traveled By

As a new missionary or as a missionary who wants to learn about orality, you might immediately ask, "Where is this all going? I know how to teach. I know the basics of orality."

In this book, I assume that the reader wants to learn about delivery, listener reception, and oral communication. I start at the beginning. In order to have the motivation to become skilled in oral work, it helps tremendously if one can grasp some basics about oral habits and about human beings in general.

People want encounter. Good evangelists and Bible teachers want it too, that is why the missionary needs to know about oral delivery, reception frameworks, repetition, inflection, gender-specific communication, embodiment, and a host of other important practical aids to understanding oral peoples.

Fortunately for you, that is not where we begin this work. Yet, that is where we are going. It will be impossible to deal with complex issues such as formulaic material: story, ballad, riddle, proverb, ritual, lament, chanting, genealogy, recitation, and a host of other oral genre without first grasping some basics about why oral peoples do what they do.

Later on, the missionary might want to specialize in individual oral genre present or predominant in any given context. For example, a more advanced question might be, "Is the controlling feature of the speech principally ritual, melodic, gestural, dramatized, etc.?"

Other specialty areas of orality concerns the fundamentals of voice: volume, tone, pitch, timbre, rhythm, register, pause, space proxemics, repetition, intensity, range, speed, tension, schematization, emotion, intensity, energy, etc. However, for the time being, we are attempting to illuminate for the reader things that are common in most oral settings and to provide a theoretical and practical basis for doing missionary work in an oral context. Many of these basic elements are things you already know but may not be aware of them.

For most western missionaries trained in a literate tradition, the first and fundamental issue is to ***break the sound barrier***. This barrier is the inability to teach and ***relate*** orally.

Americans, for example, mediate education through books, blackboards, PowerPoint presentations, and handouts. These have limited and specialized uses in oral cultures.

Anyone trying to teach orally must get over the awkwardness of hearing himself speak and repeat in ways that are not natural for literate people. A speaker often perceives himself much differently than do his listeners, and a teacher, who to himself sounds repetitive and redundant, is appreciated and applauded by people in oral cultures. Ultimately, what is awkward to the orally-trained speaker is often appreciated by the listening-dependent hearer.

Oral learners only have their memory to count on. They cannot rely on paper to do their remembering for them. Consequently, when one teaches illiterates or people who don't have paper in front of them, he/she must work from memory in order to model expected behavior. The teacher MUST have memorized the material ahead of time.

If you want people to remember without paper, you must yourself remember without relying on paper. You must memorize the material. Also, you must repeat the material enough times and in enough ways so that a learner can retain the words and ideas without much effort.

There is a certain monotony about oral delivery. It sounds excessive to the literate speaker. However, it is necessary if the hearer expects the learner to hold on to the material. The speaker is obliged to ***Break the Sound Barrier*** of literacy.

In doing so, the speaker shows real love. The oral learner says to himself, "This man loves me. He cares enough to sit here and repeat important things over and over."

That woman with whom you will be working will inevitably say to herself, "I know this western missionary knows how to read, but I appreciate her humility in not making me uncomfortable by having books around. I would be embarrassed for her to see that I am so illiterate."

Finally, this work is about oral boldness. Most Christians, even a great many missionaries, are not very good about sharing their faith. At least part of the reason is that we have not learned how to do battle in the oral arena. We put our ideas down on paper and mediate our theological battles by means of written study aids or theological journals.

In an attempt to help others overcome a similar practice of oral shyness, I have practiced and accumulated some techniques I find helpful. This book is intended to create a new foundation and perspective that permits the reader to understand why it has been difficult for many to communicate the gospel orally.

The more you have learned your faith by reading, the harder it may be for you to overcome the hardships in communicating from mouth to ear. If you have always had a text in front of you, be it on a screen, a booklet, or on paper, you are at a decisive ***disadvantage***. However, it is not the end of the world.

Use your literacy to learn the basics, then go and practice them orally. It will be difficult at first, but you will become comfortable over time in your own style of communication with the aid of print.

In reading this brief work, may you learn along with me, a man often in the prison of my literacy, to "speak boldly as I ought to speak" Ephesians 6:20. God loves those illiterate and semi-literates who live on dirt floors and under thatched or tin roofs as much as He loves the suit-and-tie-garbed Baptist sitting in a comfortable pew in South Carolina.

Paul became all things to all men that by all means he might save some. How about you? Can you become like an illiterate to win those with oral learning preferences? It's not that difficult. You are on the right road; simply, follow the Holy Spirit's indicators toward the harvest. "How shall they hear without a preacher?" Romans 10:14.

Introduction
A Written Word of Warning

This brief text is, in fact, text. It can never replace an oral demonstration and the embodied living-out that should accompany the concepts. It behooves the missionary who might read this to bow his or her head and first ask God to overcome the alphabet, the very medium that is the teacher.

Most lecturers use PowerPoint presentations, handouts, and books to explain something that must be modeled. Quite frankly, I am tired of the endless lectures and books on orality, especially by those who cannot even give a 'lecture' on orality by using the oral methods he purports to have mastered. No printed medium can capture the simple qualities of oral peoples.

Why is this the case? The answer is simple: because lectures and publications are spoken and written by high literates, trained in residential institutions that use a one way lecture method of information infusion. They refuse to renounce and escape their past.

The reader must understand that a book is a printed form of the lecture methodology. It is a one-way 'dialog.' There is really nothing dialogical about it. It cannot replace a face-to-face meeting. It is not oral. Mastering the concepts does not make one an expert in orality. An oral demonstration is better. Contact me at the address provided in the front of the book if you want an oral training seminar in which to experience the audio aspects of some of what I am talking about in this Primer.

To become an expert in orality--a servant useful to God in the context of any given ethic group--the missionary must master the oral qualities of the people, especially those qualities of the people group to which one is sent. This only happens when one loves the people.

Love is the motivator to get a handle on inflection, volume, stories, tension, rhythm, etc. It is love for God and people that push the missionary to embrace the communication methodology of the people to whom he or she is sent.

This book is my offering to you. It comes as a result of twenty years of prayerful work. When I started down this road, the road to understanding what constitutes oral engagement, I never knew where the Lord would take me.

Sitting on an island, I would literally cry tears to God asking Him why this road was so difficult. Today, I see that it is quite easy. I have tried to boil it down for you.

Orality is simple. It involves participation, embodiment, and love for people. ***It does not manage people's thinking directly.*** It lives in a constant verbal exchange with others, and it provides an avenue for God Himself to encounter us in that exchange.

Print rarely does this. There is joy in walking the journey with the simple, the poor, and the oral.

This is not to say we do not want to bring theological structure into the oral world. When it comes to the gospel, we need to replace faulty theological constructs. However, we begin with love, a love that is communicated orally.

May God grant you a superabundance of joy, the joy that I have discovered among those who want to learn about the Savior the oral way. He is the Word made flesh. He still speaks our language.

Parable One
The Etymological Shoes

Hear Now the Parable of the Etymological Shoes

Pueblo was a young Hispanic man in the rural mountains of Mexico. Someone shared the gospel with him just after the birth of his second child. He was largely uneducated and could only read a little bit.

After he was saved and baptized, he sat on one of the wooden church benches wearing his parable pants, his imaged tee-shirt, but respectfully removed his story-sombrero upon entering the building.

He sat next to many other mountain folk dressed similarly. All clutched their story-sombreros on their laps. Each Sunday, Pueblo listened to the preacher intently, admired his clothes, and had a deep desire to mature in the Lord.

Preacher Juan was educated in a training school run by Americans. He acquired his exegetical coat the first semester, his outline pants the second semester, his discursive hat the third semester, and his etymological shoes upon graduation.

Pueblo always wondered why Juan wore his discursive hat in church, but figured it was part of the ecumenical clothing of ordained preachers. It was such a fine hat. No one in church had one quite like his.

One day the preacher asked him to fill the pulpit while he was gone. Pueblo responded, "I am sorry. I have not been to seminary. Also, I have no discursive hat or etymological shoes."

"That is okay," said Juan. "You will do fine."

Pueblo struggled his way preaching through a text, but kept coming up with many stories and analogies from work, from the garden, and from the social life in town. His outline was practically incoherent.

When he preached, he did the best he could. He was full of energy. The people laughed and understood the simple text of his message. Upon leaving the church, the people really encouraged him. It was a great first sermon.

Pueblo was so encouraged that he enrolled in the local Baptist Theological Threadery. He took courses and received his exegetical coat.

Not long after, Juan was again out of town and asked Pueblo to preach. His sermon was much clearer. He could understand the text so much better.

Upon leaving the church that day, the people remarked on how much they admired his exegetical coat. This really encouraged Pueblo, and he enrolled again in the Theological Threadery.

Pueblo was diligent and eventually received his outline pants, discursive hat, and finally, his etymological shoes. He was overjoyed.

Upon graduation, Juan asked him to preach a week-long series. He donned his coat and adjusted his hat. His shoes were shined.

Night after night he preached his heart out. Night after night people remarked about his shoes, those etymological shoes. Even the pastor was proud of his young protégé.

However, deep down in Pueblo's heart, people no longer talked about his sermons. He wished he could take off his coat and put back on his parable pants and imaged tee-shirt. He missed the comfort of his story-sombrero.

He began to pray and ask God about his Threadary clothes, questioning the Lord about how come he no longer looked much like his friends and family. He received back clear word.

He looked in the scriptures and found that Jesus was not ashamed about His parable pants or His gospel of peace shoes. He wore neither discursive hat nor exegetical coat.

The next night, the last night of meetings, he showed up at the church in his imaged tee-shirt. The people were shocked. So was preacher Juan. Some criticized the young preacher, but mostly no one said a word.

Pueblo preached with all his might that night, telling story after story. The people were moved from tears to laughter to repentance. The altar was full, but that was not the most shocking thing.

At the invitation, in an unprecedented never-before-seen moment in the Mountain Baptist Church, Pueblo fell to his knees at the altar, weeping and weeping before the Lord. He placed his etymological shoes at the altar, crying out to God for mercy for having taken off his parable pants, for having covered his imaged tee-shirt, and having removed his gospel of peace shoes.

People gathered around Pueblo, praying and thanking God for the great revival He had brought to the little Mountain Baptist Church that day.

Pueblo began preaching in all the mountain villages and great crowds of unbelievers followed him wherever he went. Yet, deeper than all this, was the river of joy that flowed from his heart because he knew he was preaching like the Master.

Story Two
My Story

In 1998, I traveled to the capital city of Cayenne in the French Overseas Department of French Guiana on the northeast coast of South America to begin missionary service with my wife and three small children. Sunday after Sunday we endured French, not Creole, preaching by Haitian semi-literates. In daily life, Haitians speak Creole in French Guiana; however, in the pulpit, messages were often in French.

I literally sweated my way through the contextual conflicts, culture shock, Creolized French, and worst of all, a poorly implemented exegetical preaching model. It was then that I realized how far certain organizationally-driven homiletical practices had indiscriminately infiltrated the peoples of the world.

There in the Amazonian rain forest, my preaching model crumbled. The honest truth was that not all church leaders had the ability to do exposition, and many listeners could not read or follow the biblical text at all. The people were oral.

Moreover, it became apparent that mission settings rarely enjoyed a homogeneous, stable preaching environment. The physical context was often moving, fluid, and not conducive to detailed, expository delivery. I began to grasp the reality that there might be additional ways to develop preachers, ones which would make it possible for speakers to respond to the challenges of illiteracy.

At that point, I thought I understood communication, but I began to make discoveries that would change my life.

In taking a hard look at leader preaching styles among various groups in French Guiana, all the missiological talk about localizing and contextualizing theology seemed simply theory, theory that got lost when the previous missionaries trained their leaders in the concrete task of sermonic delivery of the gospel.

It was easy to criticize the previous missionaries for what they had done to these congregations by introducing literate standards into a world of illiteracy and semi-literacy. Unfortunately, when the time came, I found myself repeating many of the same mistakes because of a lack of alternatives. I taught them with books, too.

At that time, I was regularly training Haitian leaders. Due to extensive illiteracy among congregants, their preaching style entailed a great deal of chanting and repeating. Preachers used these practices to help those who could not read the Bible and who had difficulty in retaining key scriptures or central ideas.

Often the leader presented sermonic material with certain intonations, pauses, and interrogatives. He would walk up and down, ask questions, and even hit people who were not listening to what he had to say.

I noticed that oral formulas and stops indicated that listeners were to repeat the phrase or complete the Bible verse. It was ***oral solicitation***. In essence, the preacher was saying, "I don't know if you understand unless you repeat back to me what I just said."

Upon first hearing preaching to illiterates, I thought there was senseless repetition of easily grasped ideas. I later learned that certain patterns composed an important delivery system filled with mnemonic devices, essential to people "handicapped" by their lack of reading ability.

After I reassessed my conclusions about Haitian preaching style and came to appreciate the necessity of repetitive delivery, I then realized that there was a foreign style of expositional preaching mixed in with this Haitian variety of call and response. I also saw a people highly capable as storytellers but who were forced into a literate expositional method by the ever-encroaching French educational system and by preaching methods imported by western missionaries.

At that time, I started to construct in my mind a preaching model that was image and story-based that also utilized a great deal of Bible verse repetition. I recognized that simplified narrative style would be a step closer to the communication practices of less literate peoples than abstract exposition. I also was convinced that effective preaching needed to be tied to the biblical text as well as to the local setting.

While it was one thing to conceive a different way of preaching, it was quite another to develop *pedagogy*, pedagogy that was theologically and theoretically sound. In addition, a new preaching practice had to be appropriate to the educational ability of the people with whom I was working.

In short, I developed two methodologies: what I now call 'parabolic engagement' and 'Biblical Oral Pedagogy' (essentially patterned drilling). I piloted my ideas in several countries and eventually ended up in Martinique where I heard some of the worst preaching of my life.

Everywhere I went, there was consistent and gross failure in exposition. The preaching was stultified, rigid, and virtually lifeless in quality. It was, for the most part, devoid of any vestige of image and story. The sermons were often developed without clear reference to the biblical text and there was little focus on drill repetition so people with reading problems could learn the Bible by heart.

By contrast, I discovered that the people of Martinique loved to speak Creole, enjoyed hearing stories, and had a skillful ability to move from French to Creole and exploit the value of each language in informal communicative exchanges. Congregants in the pew, however, came to expect poorly executed, discursive French preaching as normative.

The plan to apprentice a group of people in parabolic methods of preaching grew out of a number of factors, the most important of which were my training in chronological Bible storying technique and my desire to implement a parable-based homiletic. In piloting the resulting 'parabolic engagement' pedagogy, I made some significant and unusual discoveries.

The first thing that became abundantly clear was that narrative is powerful. I, however, was not good at Chronological Bible Storying. Even more difficult was the problem of managing a storying group when I, as the leader, was not at ease.

I found story form to be more complex than anticipated, difficult for me to learn, and a far more reflective process than popularly believed. I myself, with four college degrees, could not break the sound barrier. In addition, some of my people did not easily grasp storying either. I began to ask how storying method could best be used on the field and whether it was possible to supplement it with something else that was easier for me.

I found certain types of storytelling required extensive preparation of which not everyone was capable, including myself. It appeared that almost everyone loved to hear stories, but not everyone could tell them well, especially longer ones.

I found that short stories with simple plots worked well. There were also a number of easier, quicker, and more foundational repetition practices that seemed to be more suitable for some types of discipleship settings: parables, patterned drills, and brief memorization worked well.

These discoveries brought me on a journey that has resulted in this short book. There are select aspects of orality that I wish to communicate that are foundational to the proclamation task of the missionary. They are easy to learn but will take a lifetime of fun to master.

Beginning with Jesus

Once upon a time some unsuspecting Jewish servants were sent out as a lynch mob to round up Jesus. They had difficulty fulfilling their task, because in their words, "Never man spake like this man."[1]

Spoken word delivered in the power of the Spirit by the Master of metaphor Himself left the mobsters verbally captured. Their concluding words echo Christian consensus about Jesus and represent the communicative pinnacle to which most Christians desire to rise, the point where one can say that the listener is awestruck and entranced by the message and the Savior.

The gospel message is powerful when it is spoken. It freezes the listener. God uses the oral message to draw His children to Himself.

The serious Christian searches for the door through which he might find approaches to communication that are so captivating that his message rivets the listener's attention by its simplicity and wonder. Missionaries want what Jesus had, namely, that "the common people heard him gladly."[2]

I pray that the ensuing chapters are helpful in aiding your understanding of how people listen and acquire knowledge of the living God. God has chosen simple people to communicate a great message by a foolish method: oral proclamation. "It pleased God by the foolishness of preaching to save them that believe" 1 Corinthians 1:21.

This book will help you master certain types of oral communication method and theory. Hopefully by the end you will discover that it is the message 'preached' that has the possibility of

---

[1] John 7:46.

[2] Mark 12:37.

winning the heart of sinful man.

We have no choice but to master the method of the Master. When we do, we will freeze our audiences just as Jesus managed to capture His first century crowd.

Lesson Three
The Embodiment Principle

The first principle of orality that a missionary today must learn if he or she is to enter into a culture and teach people, is the embodiment aspect of speech. Voice is owned by people. Oral speech is clothed and created by the speaker.

We do not speak for books; they speak for themselves. They stand on their own and speak only to those who take the time to read them and who know how to read.

The gospel **should** be clothed by a speaker, one who utters the message of Jesus. Consider just a couple of passages from the book of Acts, and notice how central speech is to the communication of the gospel message. The message is not mediated by print.

> And they called them, and commanded them not to **speak** at all nor **teach** in the name of Jesus (4:18).
> And now, Lord, behold their threatenings: and grant unto thy servants, that with all boldness they may **speak** thy word (4:29).
> And as I began to **speak**, the Holy Ghost fell on them, as on us at the beginning (11:15).
> But he **said**, I am not mad, most noble Festus; but **speak** forth the words of truth and soberness (26:25).[3]

---

[3] Consider also these other New Testament verses: 2 Corinthians 2:17 "For we are not as many, which corrupt the word of God: but as of sincerity, but as of God, in the sight of God speak we in Christ"; Ephesians 6:20 "For which I am an ambassador in bonds: that therein I may speak boldly, as I ought to speak"; Philippians 1:14 "And many of the brethren in the Lord, waxing confident by my bonds, are much more bold to speak the word without fear"; Colossians 4:3 "Withal praying also for us, that God would open unto us a door of utterance, to speak the mystery of Christ, for which I am also in bonds;" Colossians 4:4 "That I may make it manifest, as I ought to speak"; 1Thessalonians 2:2 "But even after that we had suffered before, and were shamefully entreated, as ye know, at Philippi, we were bold in our God to speak unto you the gospel of God with much contention"; Titus 2:1 "But speak thou the things which become sound doctrine"; Titus 2:15 "These things speak, and exhort, and rebuke with all authority. Let no man despise thee"; 1 Peter 4:11 "If any man speak, [let him speak] as the oracles of God."

The student of scripture is hard pressed to find instances in the New Testament where the message is mediated by a man with a Bible in his hand. For one thing, scriptural revelation was not in the hands of people. Second, there was a high degree of illiteracy in the Greco/Roman world. That makes the New Testament a model for dealing with evangelism in our current world where two-thirds of the world's population has an oral learning preference.

All to say, Paul used principally his mouth to change the Mediterranean Region. God prevailed upon him to go boldly with his mouth. This is the power of orality.

The message of the gospel was embodied with power by a man. He owned his words. Encounter with a living God was fully possible without paper. In fact, paper got in the way of the evangelism, discipleship, and the infusing of the power of the Savior.

This is where many missionaries fail or get hung up. *American Christianity is taught and mediated by books.* Often the missionary does not know what to do. He is out of place. He is not like his people. He has no experience teaching without the Word of God in print.

If the missionary mediates his message only with the *written* biblical text in a culture where people cannot read, people learn two things: first, the Bible is the Word of God and that the man speaking to them has respect for it; second, they will say, "We as illiterates do not have access to God Himself." Or, this is what they might be led to believe.

Evangelicals criticized the Catholics for one thousand years because they kept the scriptures from the common person. However, we do the same thing when we impose literacy on the illiterate. We make the Bible inaccessible to them.

How do we as Bible-believing Christians show a high esteem for the scriptures without alienating the illiterate or semi-literate? How can we use voice to bring about a relationship with God? How is discipleship done among those who struggle to read?

A missionary must ask herself, "What good will my books do me where I am going? Will they kill the very message I am trying to communicate?"

Before I went on the mission field in 1997, I called the missionary on the field to ask about my books. I had lots of them. My library was by all standards, enormous.

This missionary told me to bring all my books. He had no idea how many books I had. However, I took his advice, or almost.

The first thing I did was to give 1/3 of my books to the men of the church where I was serving. The second thing I did was give 1/3 of the books to the church I was serving so they could start a church library. The last thing I did was to box up about 50 boxes of books to take to the mission field.

Those books rotted in the humidity when I got to the Amazon. I also found the people to be mostly illiterate. Those who could read had such shallow doctrine, it was necessary to start at the beginning.

There was also a Bible study storage area in the city started by the previous missionary. It literally had thousands of Bible study booklets in it. 90% of those booklets had to be thrown out when I arrived because of termite damage and water damage. The books that remained were almost unusable because of mildew. While they were still usable, they were never put into circulation. All these circumstances turned out to be signs from God.

The people I served were only partially literate and, even then, did not have adequate materials in their hands. My methodology and the methodology of the previous missionary were ***book mediated.***

I found myself in a city in the jungle with a failure to be bold with my mouth in a place where those I served could care less about books. People would scurry about at 5:00 a.m. in the morning going to find work. They would come home exhausted at night and make their way to the church service, but knew almost nothing of the Word of God.

Most oral peoples have not been given the tools to internalize the Word of God because the very missionary himself who led them to the Lord did not instill in them the value of memorization or storying. This has got to change.

Embodiment: Celebrating the Savior in the Believer's Voice

Once you get rid of books, what is left? The person with the message is the only thing left that really counts. Hopefully that individual is not afraid to talk.

When someone speaks, he embodies his message. It comes from him. Bible study books, even those written by the missionary himself, do not embody the gospel. I know. I wrote five while on the field.

The books did not embody the message. The message is only embodied by people. We are the "body" of Christ. People, even literate ones, need to hear the gospel embodied in words by the speaker.

The genuineness or the shallowness of the gospel is communicated by a speaker in inflection, tears, smiles, rhythm, cadence, and intensity. Books don't do that.

Moreover, other than the Bible, the Holy Spirit does not fill books. Books cannot be heard. Books cannot respond to questions.

Even missionaries hide behind print because they do not have the courage or love to communicate verbally to lost people. People who are without the Savior want to look into someone's eyes and see that the message they are communicating with their mouth is genuine. Print can never do that.

For an illiterate, he has no memory to put on paper. He can't write things down. He relies on his mind. If you as a missionary cannot put yourself in that situation day after day, empathize and love your people to the point of putting aside your books, it is probably better that you never leave your country of origin.

Consider these verses:

> Who, being in the form of God, thought it not robbery to be equal with God: But made himself of no reputation, and took upon him the form of a servant, and ***was made in the likeness of men***. Philippians 2:6-7.

> And unto the Jews I became as a Jew, that I might gain the Jews; to them that are under the law, as under the law, that I might gain them that are under the law; To them that are without law, as without law, (being not without law to God, but under the law to Christ,) that I might gain them that are without law. To the weak became I as weak, that I might gain the weak: ***I am made all things to all [men], that I might by all means save some***. And this I do for the gospel's sake, that I might be partaker thereof with [you]. 1 Corinthians 9:20-23

Can you say, "To the illiterates, I became illiterate, so that I could win the illiterate"? Or can you state, "To those that had no experience with book learning, I became an oral teacher, so I could win the oral learner?"

As the reader will note, the final parts of this book set out a program of oral mastery required of a missionary today wanting to work among oral peoples. It greatly behooves the reader to take a serious look at his or her own lack in this regard.

Can you sustain for weeks on end, an oral pattern for learning among people who will not have books in front of them? Do you know a few basic skills in repetition, storying, or oral drilling that you can train people in the basics of Christianity?

If not, set yourselves to the task of learning oral pedagogy. Otherwise, you will never embody the message you hope to communicate. The people you serve will literally be dying to ***hear*** what you have to say.

Sermon Four

'Preaching' is a Common, Oral, Missionary Term

Statistics tell us that my denomination, the Southern Baptist Convention, is in slow decline. Many other evangelical denominations are suffering similar fates, some far more bleak. Efforts at evangelism and campaigns to improve baptisms are marginal at best. What is the reason? It is clear. We have gotten away from biblical preaching. ***'Preaching' is common, oral, gospel proclamation <u>by the entire church</u>.*** It is not, and never was, pulpit oratory.

In the New Testament, the word 'preaching' is almost never used to describe discipleship sermons within the four walls of a building. It is missionary proclamation to lost people out in the world. The audience is generally a group of people who have not been introduced to the Savior.

The ramifications of this idea are immense. What preachers do in over forty thousand churches across our denomination in America every Sunday is not biblical 'preaching', unless of course their audiences are composed of people who do not know Jesus. They may be doing sound biblical teaching, but according to the biblical witness, it is not really 'preaching.'

What a seminary might call a 'Preaching Department,' that is, a group of professors doing expositional discipleship preaching training, is vital; however, it is not 'preaching' as we read the word in the New Testament.

Evangelical preaching today does not reflect Jesus' proclamation model. Jesus would not have studied in a Theology Department ('preaching' is a sub-discipline of 'theology') to prepare for His preaching ministry. He would have refused to do that. It would have been against His theological convictions.

Having said this, were we to change our approach to engaging our world, preaching departments would have to be under the mission's faculty. The results would be dynamic.

Our proclamation model would approximate that of John the Baptist, Jesus, Stephen, or Paul. The audience would be the uninitiated. There would be far more mass conversions, and the electricity would once again flow into gospel meetings.

Mind you, this idea is not a commentary on our exegetical method, a model indisputable and vital to our growth as a denomination. However, it is an indictment on our collection technique for controlled attention witness settings and our use of the term 'preaching' for what we do on Sunday mornings.

A very elementary study of New Testament words translated into English as 'preaching' (κηρύσσω, εὐαγγελίζω, κηρύσσω, κήρυγμα, λαλέω, διαλέγομαι, καταγγέλλω, λόγος, προκηρύσσω) shows there to be an audience very much ***unlike*** our own North American church audience. When the apostles and biblical figures preached, they witnessed. They were not doing book studies and exposition to a group of individuals who already knew our Lord.

Throughout our Convention we have young men wanting to be 'preacher boys.' For them, this means teaching God's people each Sunday using expository method. Unfortunately for them, they need to be reeducated; if God has called them to preach, they ought to be missionaries, whether it be here in the local church or overseas doing pioneering.

Imagine what our denomination would look like if preaching were viewed the biblical way, as a missionary engagement endeavor. We could alter our growth plateau in one generation. We would be training all our people to do preaching in the world and not just training them to listen to the professional preacher within the confines of a church building.

By some strange twist of fate, we have come to use the term evangelism to describe witnessing to lost people, and we have left the term 'preaching' to describe what we do on Sundays. This is highly unfortunate. It was not the way of our Lord. He came preaching (Mt. 4:17).

Jesus told us to "preach the gospel to every creature" (Mk. 16:15). 'Preaching' was and still remains a missionary term.

So, how does this apply to the missionary task of orality? If in fact we understand that preaching is for everyone, then orality takes over our educational agenda. We no longer simply communicate information. We teach Christians, all Christians, how to preach.

What this means is that each and every believer is schooled in oral proclamation, that is, doing spiritual work orally. This brings a new day to the church. It also creates a new mandate for historically evangelical denominations.

We will never be the church God called us to be, especially among the oral peoples of the world, if our principal means of gospel communications is within the confines of a building by professional clergymen.

We must educate the masses of Christians to be oral communicators, to preach. Then gospel proclamation finds its proper place in the missionary task and in the church at large.

Presentation Five
Bible Storying, Orality, and Oral Performance

A critical distinction to make at this juncture in understanding orality is the difference between orality and oral performance. Oral performance is prepared delivery. Orality is a general descriptor used to define a broad collection of voice and listening realities.

For an educated person from the west, we have a tendency to formalize oral delivery in educational environments. Consequently, we take the same predisposition to the mission field and re-create the performance milieu. We prepare sermons, evangelistic campaigns, and discipleship groups like we were putting on a performance.

There is nothing, in and of itself, wrong with oral performance, but the reality is that the common person does not have the ability to perform publicly. If we want preaching, that is oral proclamation at the grass-roots level, to be owned by everyone who professes to name the name of Christ, ***we have to be careful not to make oral performance the norm for all discipleship and gospel sharing***.

This corrective does not nullify the value in oral performance. Any oral teaching is technically an oral performance. We must do it as missionaries. Some of our disciples must do it. Our ability to reproduce teachers will even greatly alter the outcome of our disciple making results. However, our proclamation practices and trainings cannot hinder our wider task of mobilization among the church at large.

Chronological Bible Storying

Chronological Bible Storying has worked extremely well in many cultures around the world. How does it work?

Existing cultural and theological frameworks become replaced naturally through repetition of Bible stories. When the missionary or teacher tells a story, there are latent lessens embedded in the story. There is also important theology that is wrapped up in how God interacts with people.

As the person learns the story, his existing beliefs and ideas are challenged. When the person learns that God punished Ham, for example, for uncovering his father's nakedness, he learns that exposing the body inappropriately is wrong.

At the higher level we might ask, "What stories are appropriate to teach in any given culture and how are they selected? What are the criteria for selecting from among the hundreds of stories in the Bible?"

The answer to this question is not simple. Usually, the teacher picks a series of carefully chosen biblical narratives to teach in succession according to select theological objectives. If the teacher wants to teach about the doctrine of God, sin, the Holy Spirit, and the trinity, he will choose the appropriate stories that inform the listener or story learner from the story plot disclosure of very specific passages from the Bible.

In turn, the teacher orally delivers the story in sequence, highlighting appropriate verses and portions of the narrative. When he is done, he might ask students to repeat parts of the story or the story in its entirety. Through several repetitions, the story and its theology is absorbed into the ideological framework of the student's mind.

Over time and through the acquisition of many stories, the broader biblical theology is absorbed by the audience. The new Bible stories displace the culturally accepted stories. With the acceptance of these new stories comes a new theology that also displaces the existing theology. Disciples are made inductively by mastering the Word of God orally.

Some Limitations with Storying among Literates

Similar methods to the one just elaborated are also used among literates. In some settings where there are people who know how to read, they may love to do storying even though they possess Bibles.

By the same token, literate peoples may not be motivated to story because they have the biblical material right there in front of them. They have no need to memorize. The print is their story memory.

This leads to a contingent issue among semi-literates trying to learn through Chronological Bible Storying. It is difficult to reproduce leaders beyond one generation using a technique for which people have no real need since they carry the stories in their hands. People see no need to memorize the stories when they have the Bible in print.

In many instances where storying is used among literates, the group is dependent upon the missionary for constant encouragement to do something that they feel is unnecessary; that is, memorize a story that is in their Bible that they can look up. Consequently, the whole system focuses on the teacher who is there to force them to do something they don't want to do. In addition, the leader may be the only one capable of creating validation, correction, and encouragement to a system that they believe is inherently unnecessary.

There is also a lingering frustration with the knowledge that the details are not reproducible. I had one woman named Johanna work for several days to learn and teach the story of Noah. She was very attentive to the details of the biblical material, but communicated to the group that it nearly wore her out for several days. She became nervous and uptight with the Word because she found it impossible to memorize all the details. It killed the motivation in the group. After listening to her complain, others thought being a story leader was impossible.

Chronological Bible Storying (CBS) was particularly difficult to bring to reproduction in the literate French context because the semi-literates with whom I was working regularly found themselves failing to reproduce ***the details they knew existed in the biblical text***.

They also knew that the oral version of the story was not the Word of God. They knew subconsciously they were not following the biblical details. This is unlike a totally illiterate culture where learners cannot validate the details on their own from the Bible.

I also got discouraged because I did not have the management skills to form a reproducible system among the literates with whom I was working. They were hard to convince.

In any performance setting, there will be people that do not want to perform publicly, especially if they have a Bible on which to rely. Some will just not want to listen to the stories. Some will refuse to repeat material. However, even if only half the people learn a Bible story, the results are immense.

In my setting, I began to realize that I had management limitations. I could not superintend their frustration well. I found my management of a group of people that was expected to reproduce longer narrative was poor. I have poor oral accountability skills. I am not alone, however.

Here is my conclusion, and I believe herein lies a lesson for anyone wishing to use storying as a discipleship medium. What this teaches is that ***narrative performance*** should not always be the norm for discipleship unless the missionary has the management skills to hold people accountable to learn extended narrative over weeks at a time. Storying can be a principle discipleship medium, but performance is mastered by very few people, even in oral cultures.

Those capable of oral performance need to be put in charge as soon as possible so that some members of the target audience are actually delivering the stories. When a leader finds he is struggling to manage the story sequence, he can alter his delivery to shorter narrative portions or to repetition drill sequences.

There are usually oral storytellers and individuals designated to retain cultural narrative within every society. Find them. We are not trying to make each and every member of our church an oral performer. What we are trying to do is have the Word hidden in their heart. These are two different objectives.

A number of years ago, New Tribes Mission put out a video entitled, *EE-Taow! The Mouk Story*, explaining a storying method used by a missionary among the Mouk people of Papua New Guinea. It has been a model for successive missionary work for those who take a systematic approach to Bible education through oral narrative methods.

The video is nothing short of amazing, but it provides an underlying assumption that is less beneficial: namely, that oral performance can be reproduced in other settings with the same results.

Professional, cultural storytellers are not a model for oral discipleship. When we take specialists in epic-style, ritual delivery and set them up as examples for simple people to follow, we have a recipe for disappointment. Professional storying is not usually reproducible among common church folk.

The resulting balance is that narrative can be used effectively when we don't expect the average congregant to be an oral performer. Rather, that average person can be a storyteller for the gospel in everyday life without being an oral performer. We can find individuals who are adept at retention to disciple people in the details of the biblical narrative, but performance is not always reproducible.

How Do We Find Balance in Storied and Non-Storied Technique?

An average, oral person functions on an aggregative, additive, redundant, and participatory model of communication, NOT subordinative or constructive model. What does this mean?

For most people, we like to communicate back and forth. We want to participate. We need to hear things over and over and over again before we learn them. Most oral learners appreciate repetition and simplicity. This is an additive model.

Unlike Hollywood Cinematic producers, oral cultures do not use tight climactic structures in their stories as we are used to them.

Orality tends to be simple, without climactic plot. That is why Jesus spoke in parables. Parables are not stories as we know them; they have flat figures and are simple in their plot.

Storying also is built on the idea of theological information collection. This must be balanced with interplay models. Storying that is properly done uses interplay and participation. It helps solidify the plot, characters, and the imbedded information.

Performance is loaded with information. Anyone who has ever done storying knows that stories need to be broken down into episodes and sub-episodes if they are to be learned. These sub-stories can be produced with interchange for learning purposes.

Performance-based models of oral storying require a certain degree of polished delivery and training. This requires time.

Oral peoples go to the fields, come back, make dinner and live in subsistence patterns. For retention to be effective among oral peoples, learning styles need to suit the lifestyle patterns of the culture.

For most, this means that average Christians need to be taught orally in small nuggets, not always in the delivery of long stories that contain large quantities of information. Whether a missionary uses narrative or non-narrative discipleship methods, oral learning must be done through the repetition of small amounts of material.

In summary, the vital principle to master is the ability to discern the amount of ***oral quantity*** to expect people to master. Also, it is important to know as a teacher what you yourself can manage in terms of accountability.

You cannot set up a performance discipleship model where quantity and polish are prohibiting factors in learning. If the oral learner has overload, or the teacher is in over his head, the leader has created expectations that are unreachable, either for himself or for his people.

In my own settings, the longer I teach in oral ways, the smaller I find my delivery material to be. Originally, I set out to teach about 150 Bible verses to my first group using drill methodology. I then reduced the number to 20 verses. I now have spilt the 20 verses into three groups of seven verses each.

Reducing the amount of material, I found I was able to focus on the critical issues appropriate to the cultural context. In asking people to master only a few verses initially, my expectations were not excessive, and the immediate success that it brought made it possible to build on a positive response among the people.

Conversation Six
Participation and the Social Quality of Orality

Inherent in orality is a people-dynamic. Many missionaries go to other countries wanting to win lost people and disciple them. Unfortunately, when those same missionaries reach the field, the very way in which they learned the faith, that is, through printed Bibles and books, is basically of marginal value for those to whom he or she is ministering.

Discipleship among oral peoples is a social exercise of verbal teaching and interaction. It is not information transfer as we have come to know discipleship.

In North America, when someone talks about discipleship, it usually involves meeting at a certain time to learn the Word of God. For a literate, this means reading and responding to ideas both in the Bible and in study aids.

However, if for argument's sake, we remove print, what form will discipleship take among oral people? How will someone learn the Word of God? How will they learn theology? How will they learn biblical constructs of how to live life without sinning?

If one has never been faced with this question, it is a daunting problem. The missionary is forced to rethink everything. In my own case, I wanted to gravitate toward the literate people on the field and teach them using the educational way I myself had been nurtured on. I did not want to develop oral discipleship pedagogy. I did not know how.

There is a death that a literate missionary must die in an oral culture. It is the death that the precious day-to-day communion he has come to love in his private devotional life with God, that is reading the Bible, will never be possible among those who cannot read. He is then faced with the question of how he will teach the spiritual disciplines and communion with God among those he serves, people who cannot read the Bible as he does.

Reading is so central to our discipleship method, many a missionary cannot function without it. Sometimes missionaries never recover from the culture shock of having to admit that literate methods don't work in all contexts.

Oral Paralysis or Oral Rhythm

There is a very real oral paralysis most missionaries face, especially in discipleship, when they get into the work among illiterates. The question is before them: "How shall I disciple a person who cannot read?" "If I form a class," one might ask, "what shall we do for an hour?"

Latent in this question is usually the assumption that discipleship is about information transfer. The social aspect of orality is minimized to the detriment of the missionary. Also, who said the discipleship session had to be an hour? My wife teaches piano. Students come for 30 minutes of apprenticeship. Time structures should be determined by local demands.

In lecture settings, social interaction is minimal. Teachers communicate truth; others receive it.

In oral settings, people want a back and forth rhythm. Teachers dialog, ask for repetition, ask questions, assure acceptance of ideas, and basically enjoy the interchange.

A missionary who refuses to accept that the people to whom he is ministering cannot fill in blanks on a paper, don't want to read a passage in the Bible because they are embarrassed about their reading inability, and don't really care that he has a Master of Divinity degree, will ultimately be frustrated and ineffective. The missionary must accommodate himself to the people.

Paul describes in Philippians chapter 2 the emptying process that Jesus went through to become a man. He humbled Himself and was made in the likeness of men. Oral teachers who are themselves literate, must humble themselves and learn how to do oral repetition, storying, oral verification, chanting, and a host of other vocal skills that are new and don't typically appear in western educational settings.

What happens when a missionary dies that death? He is usually resurrected into a whole new dimension of teaching practice, learning cultural banter, and social respect among the people he is serving. Accommodation brings with it an elevation of status among the people. They say, "He is like us. He ***talks*** like us."

Dialog Seven
Discipling in the *Hear* and Now Through Drilling

The Path to Oral Orthodoxy

In order to obtain orthodoxy on the oral frontier, there is a method of oral drilling suitable for the creation of a basic systematic theology among non-literate learners. In order to understand the path to oral orthodoxy, it is important to know the difference between narrative plot sequence and rhythmic patterns, two vastly different verbal structures used to create retention.

In order for oral learners to achieve mastery over material, the teacher can use oral patterned drilling to create immediate success and accelerated learning. Being highly selective in the choice of verses for scriptural memorization, the missionary can create a basic theological framework from the outset of his teaching ministry.

Patterned drilling method can be used as a stand-alone teaching time or it can be woven into Chronological Bible Storying by choosing theologically focal verses that encapsulate principal doctrines from appropriate stories. In the case of the latter, the story recipients are walked through a simple patterned drill to solidify the core scriptures. The focal outcome is that the believers will ". . . earnestly contend for the faith which was once delivered unto the saints" (Jude 1:3).

Orthodoxy on the Oral Frontier

With never-ending issues of syncretism, doctrinal deviance among Christian groups, and the growth of cult organizations, it is imperative that sound theology become a part of oral learning. Because orthodox frameworks among oral cultures cannot be retained by written statements of faith or doctrinal guidelines, there must be a concerted effort by missionaries and mission agencies to produce Christians that are capable of **defending sound doctrine with their mouth alone**. They need, what are essentially, oral catechisms.

In observing the churches I have been privileged to start or pastor, I have narrowed down the reason why the very disciples I have often mentored are abysmally shallow: they cannot orally defend their faith. To remedy this issue, a number of years ago I took a familiar tool of language learning, patterned drilling, and developed a methodology where it was possible to insure some degree of theological orthodoxy in my students. I wanted doctrine to be in their hearts and theologically central verses of scripture to be in their mouths. It was and remains my earnest desire that when I stand before the throne, I can "present every man perfect in Christ" (Col. 1:28).

While patterned drilling is a stand alone method, it can be employed as a teaching technique at any time with multiple purposes. The precise function I want to emphasize in the use of drill methodology is how it can be employed to create a systematic theology with or without the use of storying.

Doctrinal Vision

While narrative-based teaching methods are often concerned with salvation history and *Biblical Theology*, drill methodology is concerned with *Systematic Theology*. The Savior himself often quoted precise verses that captured theological concepts. "The stone [which] the builders refused is become the head [stone] of the corner" (Ps. 118:22); "My house shall be called a house of prayer for all people" (Is. 56:7); "I will open my mouth in a parable" (Ps. 78:2).

Selective verse memorization is a critical way for any Christian to grasp central theological concepts; it is essential for oral peoples. Illiterates have no method of theological structure-building other than mulling over what they can recall.

It should also be remembered that storying, unless it is memorized storying, is not the Bible. Narrative recounting of stories still remains a summary of the Bible. It is not the Word of God. It is for this reason that verse memorization is imperative; it is the only way they will actually have access to the exact words of God not mediated by a narrator interpreting the scriptural narrative.

Scriptural Focus

Because the abundance of words tends to relativize theological teachings so that the listener often does not know what the principal thing the speaker wants his listeners to remember, it is imperative to leave the audience with a few key scriptures that are in fact, the Word of God.

Patterned drilling is the repetition and repeating of scripture verses. It embeds the exact word of God into the mind of the listener. It is not complicated and can be learned in about 15 minutes.

The Theoretical Rationale for Oral Drilling

Patterned oral learning is broad. Drills can vary in length, style, volume, purpose, and any myriad of other factors. However, one thing is clear: *oral drilling is based on repetition and pivots on mastery.*

The nature of the oral drill is Rhythmic Sequence. Storying and other narrative methods are plot-sequenced deliveries. Both are oral. Both are effective. However, they have vastly different purposes.

Rhythmic delivery solidifies a particular concept through repetition and rhythm, not through plot disclosure. The repeating of particular focal ideas raises their importance in the mind of the listener. The fact that the speaker is forcing the listeners to repeat the concept tells the listener, "This idea is of a critical nature."

It is self-evident that narrative plot disclosure has sequence. Stories are told from beginning to end. A speaker might use phrases like, "This happened first, then this happened, and last of all, the story concluded like this." Time is the typical controlling feature of narrative plot disclosure.

Rhythmic delivery is sequential in other ways. The repetition sequence of words repeated incrementally is revelatory also, but in the sense that plot is revelatory. Each piece of syntax puts the oral puzzle together. However, the puzzle is very small. The total rhythmed sequence may only have three or four pieces. These three or four pieces are repeated ten or twenty times.

In these complementary methodologies, narrative plot disclosure and rhythmed drilling, rhythmic syntax (drilling) is juxtaposed with imaged time (narrative). Narrative is essentially a series of image clips delivered over time. Rhythmic syntax is a redundant verbal waterfall that seems to continually overflow the same spot or a wheel that goes around and around the same doctrinal axis point.

Drilling becomes in and of itself an incremental story. The story is this: "Each piece of this verse I am repeating over and over again is a foundational element to a doctrinal superstructure. It is imperative that you learn this verse so you can repeat it to yourself at any given moment that God brings it to your mind. Eventually, you will put block upon block until you have a doctrinal framework that will provide the basis of your church and family life."

Oral Accountability Structures

There are certain critical skills we need to master before we can construct living and vibrant learning experiences for oral peoples. After love, the most important skills necessary to teach orally are repetition and accountability.

The following represent the vocal groupings that may require repetition during a training session: words, phrases, stanzas, episodes, stories, storied cycles, rhythmic customs, motifs, sounds, refrains, word pictures, images, formula, and even grunts.

Whatever size the oral material is that is presented for mastery to oral learners, it is imperative to ask learners to repeat the material. This is **oral accountability**.

Oral accountability is in now-time. It is immediate. I usually begin with a question: "Will you repeat this?" "Would any man here want to attempt to say this verse by himself?" "Who would like to attempt to repeat this story?" "Who would like to repeat this episode of the story without that mistake?"

Verbal accountability is tantamount to putting someone on the spot. It is bold, but there is no substitute.

By asking people to repeat what is said, there is vocal accountability. A structure for vocal accountability needs to be put in place so that oral learners know what is expected of them.

Oral accountability structures can be varied. They can be put in place as people arrive to the teaching setting. They can be done while standing. They can be implemented for sub-groups of learners separated by sex, age, or some other variable. Regardless of how they are constructed, they must be clear and consistent.

In my own teaching, I have the tendency to degenerate into asking the group as a whole to do repetition out loud. This is not nearly as interesting as asking people to recite who are sitting in a particular location in the room, or all the men, or all the kids to repeat. Asking people to stand and speak publicly or be grouped in twos or threes is also effective. Repetition practices will naturally be dictated by the cultural structures commonly used in learning where you serve.

Accountability frequency depends on the material you are covering. You might ask first for review of past lessons. You might stop every five minutes and ask the people to repeat material. If you are working on longer stories or verses, it is a time consuming process to demand oral accountability for everyone.

Frequency is a byproduct of lesson objectives. If you are trying to master many small bits of information, oral accountability takes place very frequently. If you are explaining something already mastered, repetition will not be as frequent.

Breaking Sound Barriers: The Practical Implementation of Scriptural Drilling

There are all kinds of barriers to overcome when learning new oral patterns. The sound barriers that I find most difficult to surmount are forcing myself to speak new oral patterns that are not comfortable to me. Often they sound redundant. Redundancy to the listener is appreciated, however. It is not nearly as uncomfortable for a listener to hear repetition as it is for the teacher to repeat something he already knows.

There is also the barrier of overcoming my own self-recognition of flawed mastery. What I mean by this is that I know better than anyone that I do not have things down cold. Depending on environmental factors like noise and distractions, I may or may not be able to produce a perfect oral product. This makes me less bold in my teaching. I recognize I am a flawed master teacher.

I find myself having to push through the fear of oral mistakes. People are usually much more forgiving than I am. I know I am handling the Word of God and believe I should have things as perfect as possible.

Getting used to redundancy is not an easy task, but like any new discipline, once a person does it several times, it becomes second nature. Redundancy is a prerequisite for mastery, both for the teacher and the student. The missionary must have in his mind that this is the very Word of God; I must get it perfect. Others will reproduce my errors if I introduce mistakes by the erroneous quoting of scripture.

Oral Patterned Drilling

Oral Accountability is one of the hardest things about an oral pedagogical style. In the literate world, we give people exams, books, and ask cursory questions to see if learners have grasped the material. However, in oral settings, people expect intense oral questioning. They want the missionary to do repetition drills, to require spontaneous responses, and expect listeners to perform orally.

In order to develop good habits as an oral teacher, the teacher must himself be a master of oral accountability. The ability to solicit an oral response is not the same as the ability to lecture someone.

Anyone can speak and teach. Not everyone knows how and when to require repetition and oral response. In literate cultures, teachers tend to leave accountability until later, after the student has had the time to rehearse some of the notes. However, oral teaching demands immediate testing of the hearers. Oral response is the validation tool that assures the listeners are retaining what is being said.

You can try this in your home. Tell your child to do something. Then ask, "Did you hear what I said?" When they reply, "Yes," ask them to repeat what you said: "Could you repeat what I just said?"

Usually, the child is more apt to take you seriously if you ask him or her to repeat what you asked. This is verbal accountability.

We practice several forms of this in everyday church life in the West. At the end of a church lesson in Sunday School, there may be a set of summary questions to which the class is expected to respond. This is transferable methodology; however, in oral settings oral accountability must be the norm throughout the entire teaching or discipleship process.

Oral drill teaching might proceed like this:

"I want to talk to you about the doctrine of the trinity. What is the doctrine called?"

"The trinity," they reply.

"What is the trinity? It is the reality that God is three persons in one being."

"Who can repeat what I just said?"

"The trinity is that God is three persons in one being," someone replies.

"Can someone else repeat that?"

"The trinity is that God is three persons in one being," someone else replies.

"Let's all say that together."

"The trinity is that God is three persons in one being."

"Again."

"The trinity is that God is three persons in one being."

"Now, what does the Bible say about the trinity? I am going to teach you a verse about the trinity today. John wrote in his first letter: "For there are three that bear record in heaven, the Father, the Word, and the Holy Ghost: and these three are one." Let's learn this together. I'll say it; you repeat it."

"For there are three that bear record in heaven. Now you repeat that."

"For there are three that bear record in heaven."

"For there are three that bear record in heaven. Again."

"For there are three that bear record in heaven."

"The Father, the Word, and the Holy Ghost. Now you repeat that."

"The Father, the Word, and the Holy Ghost."

"The Father, the Word, and the Holy Ghost. Again."

"The Father, the Word, and the Holy Ghost."

"And these three are one. Now you repeat that."

"And these three are one."

"And these three are one. Again."

"And these three are one."

"For there are three that bear record in heaven, the Father, the Word, and the Holy Ghost: and these three are one. Now you repeat that."

"For there are three that bear record in heaven, the Father, the Word, and the Holy Ghost: and these three are one."

"For there are three that bear record in heaven, the Father, the Word, and the Holy Ghost: and these three are one. Again."

"For there are three that bear record in heaven, the Father, the Word, and the Holy Ghost: and these three are one."

"That was a great job."

Does this sound monotonous to you? Me too. But this is how oral people learn.

This type of talking and repeating might go on until the people are tired of doing it. At that point, it might be appropriate to lecture on the meaning of the verse and then return to a call and response process.

In whatever way the oral delivery takes place, the teacher can never be sure there is reception unless the student can repeat the material orally. This can be done in many ways. The teacher can make the first row repeat, the men repeat, the women repeat, the children repeat, etc. In some cultures it is appropriate to have someone stand and recite. In other cultures, it might be important to have the father or the leader of the people group recite publicly.

In every setting and every people group, there are standard ways of repetitive learning and oral accountability. It behooves the missionary to learn them as soon as possible. It is important to also employ them, however foreign they may feel to him as a teacher.

Immediate Success: Accelerated Learning

Oral drilling pedagogy results in immediate success. Students leave with the Word of God and it does not come back void. It accomplishes the purposes of God.

As verse is built upon verse and line upon line, students possess an internal systematic theology. Naturally, they must be instructed about that theology by the teacher; however, they themselves are the possessors of the doctrinal statement. They can quote verses to themselves or to other groups that do not adhere to a theologically orthodox doctrinal framework.

In order to create an orthodox systematic theology among oral learners, it is important to be highly selective when choosing a scripture memorization regimen. It takes about twenty verses to have a cursory, yet more or less complete, theology covering the major doctrines. My experience has shown me that people can stand about two verses per session with teaching in between. The highly repetitive nature of the delivery system makes the teaching time monotonous and difficult to do more than this. However, this envelope can be pushed by a subtle and practiced oral teacher. Consequently, the limits are subject to the style of the leader and the cultural factors present in the teaching setting.

Using Patterned Drilling with Chronological Bible Storying

When using oral drilling with CBS, it is important to choose the verses that are central to the theological framework the missionary wants to create. For example, in the creation narratives, it might be a good idea to focus on the three following verses and extract them for drilling:

Gen 1:26 Let us make man in our image, after our likeness.
Gen 2:17 For in the day that you eat of it you shall surely die.
Gen 3:21 The LORD God made coats of skins, and clothed them.

What results is an elementary theology of the trinity, sin, and atonement. If there is instruction along with the storying, the student leaves with basic biblical knowledge: he has memorized a verse about the triune God; he knows that God holds men and women accountable for their sin; and that God uses blood to atone for the sins of mankind.

While there are cultural indicators that dictate the choice of verses a teacher might want to use because of the socially confrontable sins readily evident before the eyes of the missionary (stealing, hypocrisy, laziness, murder, etc.), there are always more subtle yet more necessary underlying theological needs. Forming a systematic theology has enduring value for the long-term construction of a sound church. Correcting social sins within the church is in many cases subordinate in importance to eternal theological doctrines that give stability to Christians over a lifetime of service.

Storying should focus on the theological constructs necessary to make a basic systematic theology. The student, in just a few short sessions, should have mastery over verses that teach him about theology proper (the Father), Christology (Christ), pneumatology (the Spirit), harmartiology (sin), etc. The missionary <u>must</u> be highly intentional about certain doctrines. They are not self evident.

For example, in teaching the creation story, the fact that God Almighty is the Creator is far more evident than that He is triune. In Hebrews 1:2 it says the Father made the world through Christ. The Spirit hovers over the face of the waters. All the triune godhead was involved in Creation. It must be taught. Memorizing a verse that focuses on the triune nature of the creator God is essential. "Let us make man in our image," tells the learner that God created man special after His own tri-unity through the Son in the power of the Holy Spirit.

Hear now the parable of the two Chronological Bible Storyers

Once upon a time a missionary went up to a village to story. He was very bright and prepared a Bible story sequence that was culturally appropriate and addressed the basic issues that needed to be addressed in the village if the people there were to have a thorough understanding of the redemptive plan of God.

All the village turned out, and the men of the village were excited to begin learning the stories of the true God. They knew their own cultural stories kept them in fear of the gods of the land.

The missionary started his first story, "In the beginning God created the heaven and earth."

Many learned the first story by heart from the Book of Beginnings: how Adam and Eve sinned; how they blamed one another; how God punished them; how God placed them east of the garden. The missionary left with joy in his heart. Many people were eager to learn the story of God's love in a few days when the missionary returned.

Later that week the missionary returned to tell them the stories of Cain and Abel as well as the story of Noah. However, something terrible had happened. Only a small group showed up for the meeting.

"Where are all the people who left here with such joy earlier this week?" asked the missionary.

One of the men replied, "We have learned that you did not teach us the whole story of Adam. We have learned that Jehovah is the Creator. He is one God. In order to inherit the earth, we have to obey His laws. There is a person in our tribe that has told us he will teach us Jehovah's laws so we will not be banished from the future earth. They have decided to learn the stories from him. He told us that if we learned stories from you, we would be banished from the future earth."

The missionary was shocked but went on with his storying. Unfortunately, he left that day saddened not knowing what the next meeting would bring.

There was another missionary who also went up to an adjacent village to story. He had a similar sequence. He also told the first story. However, he did something entirely different.

When he was done telling the story, he repeated three points. His focus went like this.

"In the first episode of the Book of Beginnings," he said, "God says this: 'Let us make man in OUR image.'"

"Is God is many gods?" asked one of the astute villagers.

"No, God is three: the Father, His Spirit, and His Son. Let's say the key verse from the episode all together." He went on for ten minutes, reciting and asking the people to repeat it, sometimes alone, sometimes together. Over and over, he repeated the verse.

The missionary continued. "In the second episode of the Book of Beginnings we learn that God told Adam, "'The day you eat of it, you shall surely die.' Let's repeat that together." They repeated it over and over again.

The missionary then went on and said, "God also said in the third episode, 'The LORD God made coats of skins and clothed them.'" He again had them repeat it over and over again.

He then lectured and taught with these three verses, the theology of a triune God, the eternal penalty of sin in hell, and the shedding of blood for forgiveness. When he was done, he again had them repeat the verses, over and over again.

When he returned later in the week, he found a large crowd and had heard that some Jehovah's Witnesses had been by. The large crowd was eager to learn more stories so they could defend the faith of the triune God. They quoted verses from the episodes of the Book of Beginnings. They said, "The men who came preaching of Jehovah denied the triune God. We told them that God said, 'Let us make man in our image after our likeness.' We also told them that in the Book of Beginnings God told them they would die the death of eternal fire, and the only way to escape the eternal fire was though the blood. They testified of the help of the Spirit of God who made them bold in face of the false teachers.

The missionary was satisfied with the work that God was doing. It was a light to the dark path of the village. They were learning how to contend for the faith.

Two months later, the village possessed a clear doctrinal system of beliefs to ward off cults, witchdoctors, and divergent varieties of Christianity. Their catechism was in place.

Response Eight
Mastery

The utility of voice is clear. Each and every person carries his vocal abilities with him at all times. It requires no cost, no preparation, and no prior experience. This may seem like a simple and obvious reality, but for the Western missionary who plans campaigns and orders books, the simplicity is hard to get used to.

The immediacy of voice means that the missionary can go into a village or home and immediately start to evangelize or share. There is no need to teach reading, get books, or come back the next day. They have ears; you have a voice.

The preparatory work for oral pedagogy must be done ahead of time, however. It takes effort to memorize and master something well enough to hold other people accountable.

If you try to teach orally without having complete mastery over a simple idea, you will inevitably fall back into a reliance of print. This will teach the wrong message; namely, that you have to know how to read to get it right.

My whole ministry changed when I realized that memorizing a verse or a doctrine freed me to hold other people accountable. If I could retain something without paper, I could expect them to do the same thing. If I was paper dependent, then I found the people justifying their failure to learn something orally and to have it down cold. If I did not have it down cold, why would they live to a higher standard?

What happens in oral discipleship is that oral mastery makes recall immediate. At that point, the doors begin to open because the disciple is a walking Bible and does not need to mediate his doctrine by means of print.

When everyone in the church becomes a walking, doctrinal pillar, able to recite verses and doctrines without flinching, then the stability and reproducibility factors are virtually irreversible.

People naturally use what they can recall. If the oral process has produced mastery, then the people become evangelists and defenders of the faith more naturally.

Word Nine
The Ear as Gateway

For literate people, the gateway to understanding salvation may be their eyes. That is, they may read a text and know they are a sinner, turn to Christ, and be converted. However, for oral peoples, the only gateway they have to the gospel is their ear.

This is hard for missionaries to adjust to sometimes. The eye is a softer way to the heart. Print does not demand that I myself take a stand publicly. It does not demand that I articulate my faith. It does not demand that I share my heart. It does not demand that I risk being misunderstood. It does not demand that I give an account for myself. It does not demand that I start an exchange that is relational in nature.

When the missionary understands that the ear is the gateway, there is no place to hide, no print to mediate what God tells us to speak to others with our mouths. We are faced with our spiritual responsibility to speak the Word of God. Let us look at lifestyle changes that are necessary when we ***live*** the natural consequences of the reality that the entry of the gospel is the ear.

The Ear and Immediacy

The aural gateway is immediate. Consequently, the missionary must learn a new habit of immediacy. Gospel engagement is not put off until we can get people into a home setting. It is not the same as putting literature into the hands of someone, an action which prolongs the process of understanding.

Imagine that you are standing before someone who cannot read. There is nothing stopping you from explaining the gospel. You have your mouth; they have their ears.

They are, in fact, sinners before a just God. They are going to hell without Christ. What is stopping you from speaking? They will not find out the information any other way but your voice.

The Ear and Going Public

Print is sometimes a convenient copout. It keeps us from going public. As long as paper is doing my talking for me, I never have to own my Lord to others.

While in some countries, paper can get you killed, in most places around the globe, paper often stands in the way of a Christian who fears going public with his faith. Talking is a flawed, unrehearsed exchange, but it is so much more alive than print.

Jesus told us we should not be afraid of Him and His words. This holds true in the public arena. We must own His words and be a testimony with our mouths.

The Ear and Personal Accountability

With print and western-style discipleship, there is very little accountability in the immediate. However, in the oral world, we can immediately ask questions.

"Did you understand what I just said? Do you believe what I said? Do you want more information? What do you think you should do about this truth? How will this affect your family? Do you understand the results if you reject this message?"

This sort of accountability only exists in the present. It may happen again tomorrow, but at that time tomorrow, it will again be the present. The time is now. We must demand acquiescence to the Savior of the gospel.

In my own journey toward evangelism, this has been the hardest lesson to learn. I have a mandated call from God to hold people accountable for what they hear.

In American culture, we fear treading on the feet of someone else's personal convictions. We do not want to upset cultural norms or personal myths on which people are leaning for false comfort. Their reaction is sometimes more than we can bear. Consequently, we allow them to go on in their unbelief.

However, when we stand before God, He will ask us about our mandate to share Jesus with lost people. He will say, "You had the Savior. You had the tools, namely, your mouth. All you lacked was the will to open the tool box."

Every day there stand before us countless individuals with two ears. God gifted them to receive the message, at least physiologically. Whether the message enters their heart is the Holy Spirit's responsibility. Ours is simply to be the instrumental means of sharing God's message.

The Ear and Response Clarification

One clear advantage to speaking and engaging oral people is that it is possible to immediately clarify problems. If someone has a question, you can take the time to talk more about the point in question.

Print does not have that option. Paper informs those who can read. It does not answer personal-type questions for anyone, especially for those who can't read. For illiterates, it answers none of their questions.

Orality has its decisive advantages. It provides a platform for personalization. People who employ oral methods must shake predispositional strictures that are a byproduct of literacy. For instance, a literate person might not be inclined to seize a question as a means of entry into a theological discussion that could ultimately bring a person to salvation.

Consequently, people who have the habit of being behind computers, books, or print don't usually capitalize on the very real advantage they have in oral settings. We must use the flexibility available when talking to people to pursue the conversation to the depth it needs to be taken.

The Ear and Personal Relationship

However shallow or introductory a conversation may begin, it is still the first step toward something deeper. Speech is invitational. Its very nature is an exchange.

For the missionary, the death-knell to breaking out of past print-bound habits is thinking, "I need to get these people into a controlled-attention witness setting where I can ***really*** talk to them." There is no better time than the present.

Oral instruction is in the here-and-now, or better, the *hear*-and-now. When the first word is spoken, the invitation is put out there, and a missionary should capitalize on it.

Sure there is flexibility, embodiment, and accountability in orality, but first there is a sort of mystical relational element that must be acknowledged. When someone speaks to me, I start to form a bond, however cursory. It is something to respect.

Print makes no commitment and can form a bond with no one. When I speak to a person, however, I have brought our spirits within proximity to one another. Since I am a believer and the Spirit of God abides in me, the other person is coming in contact with God's ambassador.

I cannot deny the sanctity of this reality. Nor can I deny its power. Every missionary must ask himself if he is God's agent for kingdom purposes. Talking to people is the most basic element in the orality equation. It is the sanctified invitation to transformation. We must decide to walk through that door.

Talk Ten

The Oral, Cultural Container

Orality is a vast repository of cultural detail. It contains most of the culture of any given people group. Sure, there are rituals and enactments, advertising and print, habits and actions, but the vast majority of cultural forms are in the speech of any language.

This is not theory, however. It is the open door to the gospel.

When someone opens her mouth, she speaks volumes about herself, her preferences, her fears, her tendencies. It is something to which we need to pay attention.

Within any spoken language there is more than an oral invitation to relate, however; there is also a key to cultural bondage, confusion, and pain. Cultures have tendencies, decided pathways that have guided them for years.

It is imperative that the missionary who speaks to someone, hear the cry of the slave in bondage hidden in the speech communication. Words are transmitters of buried culture.

If in fact speech is a mine, then the Christian should be a miner, descending the depths of the shaft to seize hold of the nuggets that provide a framework for missions. There are within the speech habits of any people, basic oral tendencies that are doors to concepts and habits that form the makeup of a given group.

One thing that I did in my first year as a missionary is get a hold of James Spradley's, *The Ethnographic Interview*. In the course of my missionary career, I conducted hundreds of oral interviews using the suggestions in that book.

About 150 of the interviews I did were either audio recorded or written in the published ethnographies I wrote for the mission or for my doctorate. Interviewing was one of the most personally rewarding things I did as a missionary, not because I collected information, however useful that may have been, but it provided a framework for gospel proclamation and personal relationship.

Many missionaries today want to get their information from books. It is almost impossible to learn about current cultural practices from the Internet or from print. Oral communication produces a living classroom of cultural values.

When I was 19 years old, I lived in Israel for a year. I was taking Hebrew in classes twice a day. But each day at 3:00 p.m. in the afternoon, I hit the streets.

Books are great, and they have their place, but no one can take away from me the hours I sat at the Western Wall with old, retired Israeli soldiers just shooting the breeze in Hebrew. I learned more for two hours each day on the street than I ever dreamed of learning in Ulpan language classes.

I did the same thing in Greece while studying Greek in Macedonia one summer. The Greek people, like most orally inclined ethnic groups, are chatty. They love their culture. They will talk at length about themselves.

Why would anyone want to learn from a book when books are written about people? The source is the people themselves and their language. There is no substitute.

Authenticity for an aspiring missionary is learned in the crucible of barefoot language learning. No missionary can live without it; it is just a question of how deep is the water in which the missionary wants to swim? My suggestion is to get in just as deep as you can.

Picture Eleven

Controlling Metaphors and Definitive Cultural Images

Within every oral culture is a vast pool of images and metaphors that silently control thinking and, by extension, action. These thoughts flow in the symbolic arena of men's minds and come out in speech. The key is to seize on them. They move cultural understanding forward for the missionary.

Oral language is a cultural receptacle that helps the missionary know why a people are doing what they are doing. Images and speech figures need to be dismantled.

Speech contains archetypes and historic predispositions. By talking to people in another language in which we were not raised, we find out what is important to a particular ethnic group, who their gods are, what they hope to experience, who or what they are afraid of, and why they do what they do. There is no substitute for this.

When I went to French Guiana as a missionary during our first term, I realized that there was a lot of talk about spiritism. I tried to collect a vocabulary but found it difficult to put together a local theology of spiritism.

To clarify things for myself, I wrote out about fifteen terms I knew for witches, voodoo, sorcery, incantation, etc. I took them to several people and asked them to explain them to me by arranging them. What I discovered was amazing.

"Could you arrange these for me and then explain them?" I would ask.

"Sure," came the reply. "These are French terms. These are Guianese Creole. These are in Haitian Creole. This is a term the Amerindians use. These terms have come across the border recently since there are a lot of Surinamese and English Guianese coming down from up north."

Many of the terms referred to the same things or were synonyms. Others were in a world by themselves. They held distinct meaning in the culture. Talking it out with the locals was worth years of mistaken observation.

Within the language of a culture, however, are special words and concepts. Often these are image-based. They may be symbolic in some way and could be represented by animals, trees, birds, fictitious things, or people.

The cultural symbols that are orally repeated are extremely important to understand. These images provide a means for people to relate to one another and often mark some kind of universal experience.

Socially defined sign is part of a common knowledge base. In American culture is it pioneering individualism symbolized by any number of archetypal metaphors: the gun, the covered wagon, the small business owner, etc.

If someone were to come as a missionary to Cecil County, Maryland where I live, and he tried to preach gun control law along with his gospel, he might as well pack up and go home. Every man in the county hunts with three or four guns a year, depending on what season it is. A missionary from the outside might think it is a violent county filled with violent people if in fact that outside individual comes from a culture where guns are illegal.

The receptivity of an audience to a speaker will be greatly helped by that individual's grasp of the controlling metaphors and archetypes in a culture. The task of unpacking cultural images is of vital importance to communication in any language or geographical region.

Situation Twelve

Flexibility and Contextualization: All Things to All Men

Print is unchangeable. Oral methods are fluid; they change with the context.

Books are static, inalterable. They don't answer questions. They don't respond. They can't put their thoughts in new lights based on a given situation.

The voice, however, shifts and reacts. It modifies and constructs based on all the factors in any given speech setting. This is a great advantage over printed media.

The voice can adjust to contexts, questions, handicaps, and needs. Voice permits possible immediate shifts in discourse type that print does not. For example, it may be natural to go from assertion to prayer to story to interpretation and back again. Ambiguities of vocalized discourse are natural. Interaction with context becomes the norm.

A person entering into a mission setting must understand that the people he is trying to reach are not concerned about the doctrinal perspective of the published material. Rigidity will not work. What they want to know is if the missionary can relate to them, love them, and sit and talk to them. Oral methods have the flexibility to show love by adjusting to need.

Paul put it this way: "To the weak became I as weak, that I might gain the weak: I am made all things to all [men], that I might by all means save some. And this I do for the gospel's sake, *that I might be partaker thereof with [you]*" 1Co 9:22-23.

Paul says that when he becomes like his hearers, he becomes a partaker with them. In becoming like someone else you share with them in perspective. The principle is that contextualization brings identification.

Orality is always contextualizing, always shifting. It rarely has the rigidity of printed order.

Consequently, the missionary does not want to go in and impose print-based standardization. Bible stories and the exact Word of God in memorized form will do that in its own time, certainly faster than the missionary could do on his own with sociological controls.

To win someone to the Lord, the task is to first identify with the people you are trying to reach. In our discussion context, this means becoming oral.

How does one become oral? If a given ethnic group sits around for hours talking, you sit around for hours talking. If they teach by repetition, you teach by repetition. If they transmit their tradition around the fire, you transmit your teaching around the fire. If they interject small words after every sentence to show they are listening, you interject small words after each sentence to show you are listening.

If your objective is to win them to Christ and disciple them, you have to ask yourself, "How will these people hide the Word of God in their heart?" How can you expect them to memorize scripture and Bible stories if you do not do it?

A missionary cannot be reading dependent in an oral culture. You must memorize what you are trying to teach. If they have nothing in their hands, what kind of teacher are you if you read out of the Bible?

This is not to say you don't show the example of the Word of God by bringing it with you. Surely, read from the scriptures. However, if you do not model for them the kind of disciple you expect them to be, they will never be that kind of disciple. You have to be a memorizing disciple before they will ever want to be a memorizing disciple.

If in their culture important things are memorized, memorized cold, what kind of disciple will they think you are if you don't memorize things cold? You are to them a lousy disciple. They will say of you, "He does not think high enough of His religion to memorize even basic sayings from the book he says comes from God!"

Context Thirteen
Contextualization through Narrative and Repetition

You will discover, if you have not already, that an oral culture has a different hierarchy of values. It values narrative, not lecture.

Oral cultures appreciate story. It reflects who they are and how they live. It is the common way to transmit beliefs, expected behaviors, and hopes.

A benchmark article about "The Narrative Quality of Experience" was written by Stephen Crites in the *Journal of the American Academy of Religion* in 1971. He points out that people live narrative.

If a missionary speaks in narrative, he is speaking what people live. We are temporal; that is, we move in a time continuum. Actions are sequential. This is why when people talk in narrative formats, we perk up. It reflects our experience.

Oral peoples are not different; in fact, they are all the more quick to perk up because they do not have a highly developed capacity to objectify their thoughts as literate people do.

Also, oral peoples value repetition in a learning setting, not necessarily novelty. We like to hear something new all the time. Oral cultures appreciate repetition when they are trying to learn. It helps them remember what they cannot put on paper.

Even small children, who are essentially oral, love to watch the same videos over and over again. Why? They do it because they value repetition. Experiencing things is a way of solidification. They enjoy the solidification process.

High literates, which most missionaries are, do not enjoy repetition. They value novelty and don't like repeating things excessively. This was my problem with Haitian preaching. I could not stand the Creole form of call and response. It was annoyingly repetitive, at least at first.

A missionary has to die two basic deaths to become oral. The first is the death of thought objectification and the second is the death of deep thinking. Thought objectification dies and is raised to life as narrative. Deep thinking dies the death and is raised to life as simple repetition.

Without narrative, values cannot be transmitted. In the same way that theology in the Old Testament is, for the most part, transmitted in the historical books through narrative, oral cultures transmit their cultural belief systems through narrative.

Narrative contains theology. A missionary uses his stories to replace and displace earlier stories to recreate a theology that is biblical.

Second, the missionary's deep thinking, advanced levels of theological training, and thought objectification must give way to repetition. That is, the habit to turn inward to deep reflection MUST be replaced by the habit to turn outward to repeat over and over again the simple things of the faith.

Objective thought is selfish and concerns the missionary. Often missionaries become imprisoned in their own minds with the myriad of cultural conflicts. It becomes imperative to turn deep thought into simple repetition that is externalized and others-focused.

The people you serve are simple. They will appreciate oral repetition, simple repetition. They do not know what you are going through in your life, but they do know you care about them when they hear you repeat things over and over again.

Once a concept is in place through repetition, higher thinking becomes possible. It is amazing how fast the transition takes place. Yet, the process in getting there is repetition.

Lesson Fourteen

The Parable: THE Fundamental of Missionary Engagement

Since we do not want information to replace practice in missionary training and service, this small lesson addresses one fundamental aspect of oral pedagogy: the parable. It was Jesus' method. It should be ours, especially when we want to engage lost people who are uninitiated with Christianity.

Basic Oral Pedagogy

The place to begin in oral pedagogy is the engagement. Oral engagement is best done in a figurative way. Jesus used parables.

I place here the importance of parables because it was Jesus' way. We have abandoned it in modern evangelism practice. We must return.

The justification for parabolic preaching is simple: it is what Jesus did. In almost thirty years of international education, global travel, and overseas mission work, I have never heard a single church speaker, either in the United States or in a foreign country, preach a sermon that, in any way, remotely resembled the parabolic delivery style of Jesus.

Considering I have heard about 10,000 sermons in my life, this is an abysmal statistic. The obvious conclusion is that we have chosen to not do what Jesus did. We are also not seeing the evangelistic results that He saw. It is no wonder that 70% of all churches in the Southern Baptist Convention, for example, are plateaued or declining.

As a consequence of this rather serious flaw in leadership training around the world, I set out to develop parable creation methodologies for preachers. More specifically, I have spent the last 5 years developing straightforward parable development training for those who could not read well. Below is an introductory primer in parable creation that will take ten minutes to read; however, it will take you the rest of your life to master.

Parabolic Engagement

This is what Mark says about Jesus' ministry in Mark 4:34: "But without a parable spake he not unto them: and when they were alone, he expounded all things to his disciples." Engagement was narrative parable delivered to the uninitiated; discipleship was expository discourse delivered to the saved community.

Jesus was the master preacher. It probably goes without saying that we should be more like Him in our speaking habits. However, we often complicate our engagement process with complex discourse. Jesus was much more direct.

The Savior had a simple way of communicating profound truth using common objects and scenarios. These thoughts are a synthesis of a twenty-year passion to recreate His method in a way that is simple enough for people to learn in ten minutes. It has been my calling before God to make this accessible to the average person. It has cost me many years of isolation and tears. May it help you change the world for God's glory.

The ensuing four techniques represent the most essential ways to create parables to illustrate biblical ideas. In the same way that parables captivated the poor and drew people to the desert to hear this simple Teacher, they can yield similar results in your ministry.

The Savior showed accommodating love for people in the way He talked with them. We should also. Unfortunately, the style that appears so simple is not so easy to reproduce without help. I have struggled for years to identify the essential ingredients of parable construction and delivery.

Below are several ways to empower your oral engagement process through parable construction. These simple methods will help you not only illustrate the textual idea in the Bible you focus on, but also assist you in grabbing hold of the wayward human will.

The following parable-construction techniques can work in pulpit ministry or street preaching from the Bible and assume that the speaker has already done exegesis and has isolated the preachable subject and the illustrative crux of the text.

Moral Polarizing. The parable is a tool that divides the heart. When Jesus used it, it was not an entertainment device. It was certainly not narrative preaching as we know it today, although some would like to think so.

Jesus placed people in a moral dilemma. He gave them two choices: right or wrong, heaven or hell, good or bad. There was no middle ground.

He asked them if they were on the wide road or the narrow one, in light or darkness, among wheat or tares, like the Samaritan or the priestly hypocrites, like a self-righteous older brother or a repentant prodigal, guided by the divine master or mastered by money.

Parables in preaching create a moral crisis. They divide the heart, leaving one's choices subject to the conviction of the Holy Spirit.

Anyone wanting to create a polarizing parable should identify the two opposite choices and then create a story intending to lead the listener to choose the lifestyle that God would approve. The parable would begin with phraseology similar to Jesus' parable of the two men who went up to the temple to pray: "Once there were two church members . . ." or "In a town there lived two sisters . . . ." The parable would then briefly sketch two behaviors. One, of course, is the godly and preferred choice.

Cyclical[4] Parables. Jesus often told parables using cycles or brief episodes. These are similar to childhood stories most of us heard during our youth: The Three Bears, The Three Little Pigs, or Three Billy Goats Gruff.

In cyclical parables, there are a series of vignettes that demonstrate several levels of obedience or types of individuals. For example, in the Parable of the Sower there are four types of soil, each yielding varying results. Varying types of ground represent different types of people. Among other parables with clear cyclical plots are the parable of the minas and the parable of the laborers in the vineyard. Jotham's parable in Judges 9:8-15 is also a very fine example of a parable with cycles.

Parables that stratify individuals through varying levels of obedience are simple to create. Once the preacher locates what he

---

[4] The term 'cyclical' belongs to Françoise Tsoungui, *Clés pour le conte africain et créole* (Paris: Conseil International de la Langue Française, 1986).

wants to illustrate, he finds two to four other secondary or poor choices to contrast the ideal choice.

Were one to preach on Acts 6 and the selection of godly deacons, for example, it would feasible to create a brief story with three or four fictitious deacon candidates that might all be flawed in some way. However, the deacon God would want would certainly be the one man filled with the Holy Spirit and faith.

Image Parables. There are a number of very curious verses in the gospels that show that not all parables are stories. In spite of arguments over the definition of the word 'parable', parables are often single images or extremely brief narratives without plot.

Image parables are forceful and shock the listener with their simplicity. The kingdom of heaven is like leaven or like a mustard seed. If the blind lead the blind, both will fall into the pit. The gospel writers use the term 'parable' to describe these simple pictures. There is no reason why we cannot follow Jesus' example by using verbal images that force listeners to examine their belief systems

Original parabolic images are created using analogies from the context in which the audience lives. For example, while preaching on the tongue in James 3, the preacher might find similar images to those of James. Instead of using bits, fire, rudders, or animal tamers, the speaker can move to application by analogy and ask husbands if their tongue is like a tornado that touches down in town and rips through the neighborhood. Tongues might be like termites that destroy the beautiful home unnoticed or like a tsunami that comes ashore unannounced.

Negative Parables. Often Jesus used negative parables or shockingly bad examples. He did this by demonstrating truth or correct action by picturing the opposite. Unfortunately for those who listened to Him, they often found themselves just like the person or thing He described. He talked of evil tenants and rich fools because they were so common. They were also not well-liked. Who would want to be one of those people?

Jesus told us that if we see eagles, we might find a dead carcass. We should not be surprised when Jesus comes back because, after all, the circling eagles gave away the future reality that was just around the corner. Eagles meant death, judgment, and by extension, the return of the Messiah.

When missionaries are at a loss for a way to picture correct action or proper thought, it is often possible to come up with a myriad of poor alternatives. These can be woven into a teaching as contrastive elements that demonstrate by negative example what the scriptures are really trying to say.

Oral Engagement Using Parables

There is a great deal of talk about narrative methods today. However, a parable is neither a complex narrative nor an illustration. Parables have 'flat' characters that are not complex. The story line of a parable lasts between five seconds and two minutes. Parables do not usually have much suspense, although some cyclical parables might build into a brief climax.

The danger of using modern-day storytelling technique is that we might be inclined to follow our culture and believe that a good story works similarly to a parable. Often times a story does not force a moral choice. Similarly, story tension and suspense are not usually part of delivering a parable. Parables have vastly different objectives and results. They concern moral confrontation and correct choices.

When a preacher uses a parable he may be dissatisfied with the lack of storied force. The parable lands abruptly. However, that is the point. While resolution in Western-style stories is rather satisfying, parables are often unresolved, even harsh.

If we are to ever bring people to a saving knowledge of Jesus, it is impending upon us that we show them the futility of competing alternatives. This is the power of the parable.

Unveiling the heart is not a delicate process. It is often a brutal reality. So while the wicket gate appears mighty narrow, it is an infinitely better choice than the alternative. In reality, we do people a favor by clarifying and simplifying what the devil has fogged up. Jesus gave us the tools for proper illustration of His word. They are simple and clear. There is no need to complicate them.

Two missionaries went on the field to preach. One took his complicated outline, full of subordinations. His manuscript was dotted with illustrations he had downloaded to his flat panel monitor. He said to his oral people, "People, I have three points I would like to make today." His audience was duly impressed with his clarity.

The other preacher would not take his eyes off his people. He opened his mouth and said, "Dear folks, two congregants went to the church to pray . . . ." The people listened with intensity. They sat in astonishment.

I tell you a truth; the missionary that spoke in parables had a full invitation and went to his house justified rather than the other.

Performance Fifteen

Storied and Non-Storied Presentation

Most missionary storying performances are constructed around systematically memorized discipleship collections; that is, missionaries carefully select a series of biblical stories to tell the narrative plan of redemption or some other critical theological idea. However, there is something that needs to be said about the limitations of story performance as a discipleship medium.

Oral peoples communicate around practices and need. In order to tell a series of stories, there needs to be controlled attention settings. Once there is a controlled setting, one enters into the performance milieu and one is out of the domain of common orality.

When I was introduced to Chronological Bible Storying (CBS) by Jim Slack of the International Mission Board of the Southern Baptist Convention, it confirmed some basic premises I had held for years since my doctoral education in rhetoric. Narrative is a powerful, but underutilized, tool.

I found my own training in CBS method to be difficult to master. I realized that I could not do it well. I found myself 'crippled' by my literacy and my inability to recount narrative.

The problem was not in the method. It is being used in venues around the world with enormous success thanks to the efforts of select individuals who have a passion for communicating the Word of God.

In my implementation of the method, I found myself going down a different road, however, one that involved teaching smaller portions of scriptures to our churches. My own inability to recount longer narratives forced me to develop a non-storied, oral discipleship method.

Why was it hard for me to story? I found that I could not remember important details. Also what was said by me was hard to reproduce outside a controlled setting.

The basic reason was length. The oral performer has to prepare for a significant amount of time to do what needs to be done. It cannot simply be copied by listeners on the fly and taken out into the world, at least not by most listeners.

Storying requires serious preparation to be reproducible at a quality level. This is the limitation.

Having said this, storying is essential for introducing theology and displacing false ideas about God. Consequently, storying must be done in order to introduce people to correct theology, holy conduct, and divine expectation.

Biblical stories displace existing stories. In so doing, biblical theology displaces pre-existing theologies. Along with the displaced theologies go destructive actions and thoughts.

In the same way that stories communicate ***biblical theology***, I believed that there needed to be a complementing method that could help create ***systematic theology*** in the life of the oral learner. What resulted was a Bible verse learning program. Both storying and single verse repetition provided a balanced approach to discipleship among oral peoples.

Since much has been said about storying in other places and by other individuals, and since I am not an expert in storying, I prefer not to deal at length with storying methods. I want rather to present a method for creating systematic theology in the lives of hearers.

This method is a performance-based model just like storying. However, it has a few basic elements that are highly reproducible: Speaking, repetition, mastery, and duplication.

This type of oral training technique is based on a central habit every missionary learns when he or she learns a foreign language: repetition. It is a drill-based methodology.

What is repetitive, oral training technique?

Oral training technique is a group of methods used to instruct oral learners using repetition and on-the-spot verbal accountability. It involves the use of spoken teaching routines.

In oral training the teacher assists the oral learner in processing through the three stages of the memorization progression: acquisition, recall, and retention. He does this by speaking out loud and by repeating small bits of information over and over and over again. He is led in this process by an oral instructor that has been trained in the basic *techniques of oral transmission.*

How simple is oral training technique from the teacher's point of view?

Oral training technique is extremely simple. However, it usually requires relearning how to teach. **Oral transmission** (the teacher's oral delivery habits) involves his or her demanding and **expecting oral recall** from the student. Recall methods are usually a combination of reciting, prompting, asking questions, finding volunteers, correction, motivation, and a number of the substitution exercises. The entire learning process consists of three stages: 1) Talking; 2) Repeating; 3) Mastery.

Oral learning (that is, from the student's perspective) involves repeating and answering the prompts of the teacher. Consequently, the teacher must be an oral teacher. Most Americans are not accustomed to *oral accountability in the immediate.*

In oral pedagogy, the accountability habits of the teacher determine the effectiveness of the overall discipleship process. The teacher must memorize, recite, demand on-the-spot repetition, and correct the faults of students. Mastery will not take place outside the classroom without a teacher, simply because there is nothing written to carry away. Oral learners have no information storage medium other than their memory. Consequently, it is imperative that the teacher be a specialist in powerful, oral transmission.

How do I re-learn how to teach?

Jesus was God, but yet He became man. "And the Word was made flesh, and dwelt among us . . ." John 1:14. In the same way, we who are high literates must become oral. "Therefore I endure all things for the elect's sakes, that they may also obtain the salvation which is in Christ Jesus with eternal glory" 2 Timothy 2:10.

The first step in re-learning how to teach is to assess your own pedagogy, that is, the way you teach. More carefully, you must assess your pedagogy acquisition, that is, how you were taught to teach. What you expect by way of results is likely what was expected of you. How much talking you expect your students to do is a result of both your personality and how you yourself were taught.

In oral pedagogy, the student should talk about 1/3 the time. For anyone trained in a highly literate classroom, this is an enormous shift in the teacher/student talking ratio. Student repetition requires that the teacher ***expect*** the student to repeat, correct, and master the material orally. The teacher actually is quiet while students repeat, fill in the oral blank, correct, and master the verses.

To assess your own dexterity in teaching orally, it helps to evaluate the level of student passivity in the learning model you acquired up until this point in your life. How much time do students sit in silence? If you take away their pens and books, what would your students be doing while you are teaching?

After you have assessed your pedagogy, then you must unlearn much of it. Often it is hard for a person with the gift of teaching to realize that they need to be quiet enough to see if the students are actually learning. This is a radical shift from western classroom method. We are pursuing oral mastery, not teacher lecturing.

The teacher must embody what he/she is teaching. There must be identification of the teacher with the substance of the teaching. It helps if the teacher can employ speech and emotion that reflect the meaning and the emotional export of the verse. For example, if the verse is about compassion, the teacher should teach with compassion. If it is about witnessing, the teacher should embody Spirit-led boldness.

Is there a particular type of content that works well with oral training technique?

Among oral peoples, most teaching should be highly repetitive with oral accountability. Consequently, there is not one particular type of content that works better. One can even improve one's Chronological Bible Storying using proper oral technique. This author has effectively constructed non-narrative, theological frameworks in the congregations in which he has served. The type of training done by this author is called Biblical Oral Pedagogy (BOP).

What is Biblical Oral Pedagogy (BOP)?

BOP method is a way to teach Bible verses to learners using strict oral accountability. It enables the missionary to help listeners to construct a ***systematic theology*** simply by memorizing key Bible texts.

It does not employ narrative technique, but rather makes use of extensive repetition and several other spoken teaching routines.

The purpose of BOP method is to provide a ***biblical focus*** to an oral learner's theological framework. The missionary first isolates critical Bible verses that are needed to construct a ***growing*** conceptual framework, then teaches them in stages to the individual, church, or group. This incremental staging of the theological development is called the BOP Ladder. It is a mean of helping oral learners construct a cursory, yet complete, systematic theology.

In the BOP Ladder, the learner processes through an ever increasing repertoire of verses using the three stages of the memorization progression: acquisition, recall, and retention. He does this over and over and over again with small bits of information.

Since this is not Bible Storying, it can be used to teach non-narrative portions of the Bible. This enables the missionary to focus on the more didactic portions of scripture that are important for building disciples with a balanced theology. ***It is particularly important for teaching the Pauline Epistles.***

Once the learner has achieved mastery over Bible verses and their meaning, he is then able to teach another learner what he himself has learned. Each learning unit should be about 20 minutes in length, but instructional time will vary according to circumstances and people group.

What is the *content* of BOP?

The content of the BOP method is only the Word of God. The student is basically doing Bible memorization, albeit, carefully engineered to construct a basic systematic theology. Steps in the learning ladder are thought out in advance. This process involves choosing Bible verses that are important to ground the learner in the foundational doctrines of their new faith. Verse selection by the instructor can build bridges, break down cultural barriers, and establish the believer in the "first principles" (Hebrews 5:12). A sample ladder is provided at the end of this manual.

What are the basic elements of BOP?

Naturally, your oral pedagogical model must be modified to fit the culture; however, there are two basic elements that cannot be eliminated from the oral transmission process.

Teacher Memorization/Speaking → Student Repetition

If we break this down further, a more realistic model looks like this:

1. Teacher Memorization
2. Teacher Oral Delivery
3. Student Repetition
4. Teacher or Student Correction (if necessary)
5. Student Repetition
6. Mastery
7. Teacher Reproduction

How much memorization must I do?

It goes without saying, that the Teacher MUST be a student of the Word of God. In oral learning, this means he must have memorized the texts he is about to teach. This is a non-negotiable element of oral pedagogy. A teacher cannot rely on the text. It will be a good idea to have a Bible in your hand, but you must be able to repeat Bible verses verbatim. Your failure to do so will result in the distortion of the scripture.

A leader must model the kind of behavior he expects. If you expect less literate peoples to have a theological framework in their head, you must have one in yours. If you expect excellent recall of your students, you must have excellent recall. You must practice the excellent oral pedagogy you want them to implement in their discipleship process with their families.

The extent to which you master the content will directly reflect on the level of accuracy your students will have. Consequently, you must take your time and do very small units over and over again. If you do not memorize well, don't be discouraged! You are just like most people. You are the perfect teacher. You will likely go slowly enough for good learning, that is, if you make a commitment to memorize the Word of God correctly.

What do I do with people who do not like on-the-spot learning or who do not like to memorize scripture?

You MUST expect the student to practice the verses on-the-spot. There should be some springboard verses that are easy to master. This gives people confidence to continue in the process.

On-the-spot pedagogy does not necessarily mean singling individuals out. Having said this, I like to do it anyway. It usually creates a fun dynamic if the person who is called upon is praised for their effort.

Naturally, no one likes being corrected. However, the ability to receive correction is a sign of humility and a willing heart. Students who enter your learning domain must recognize immediately that they are expected to fit their behavior into the mold of the group.

People tend to renegotiate their personal learning habits on-location in the teaching setting. That is, they modify their apprenticeship according to teacher expectations. If everyone is repeating, they will learn to repeat as well. We want to maximize the power of the collective orality of the group.

Collective orality in group repetition emphasizes the unity of the learning process. It shows those listening (and refusing to repeat) that this group of people is together in their learning process. It shows collective love for God's Word. It says, "We're in this together."

How can I reinforce the oral process inside and outside the learning area?

There are several ways to reinforce the oral process. There should be multiple levels of accountability partnerships. It is possible to create drill partners or teams of individuals to do repetition exercises. However this takes place, there should be some kind of peer improvement process. Those who achieve mastery should be strategically placed to multiply their skill. In addition, everyone should be expected to go home and work with their family to create oral disciples if the context permits it.

"But sanctify the Lord God in your hearts: and [be] ready always to [give] an answer to every man that asketh you a reason of the hope that is in you with meekness and fear" 1 Peter 3:15.

After I have memorized verses, what does a BOP 'teaching time' look like?

In diagramming the flow of an oral apprenticing model, there is a cycle that moves from delivery to repetition to mastery. It can be pictured like this:

Delivery→Repetition→Correction→Repetition→Mastery

In the background, there is always a climate of oral accountability. It is practiced with immediacy. This climate must be established from the outset. A good way to frame the verbal expectations is by telling the students that you will speak and they will repeat. Tell them you expect a growing posture of boldness in their repetition. These are some of the essential elements of the drill:

- Teach them the first verse.
- Demand repetition out loud.
- Require adequate volume, speed, and accuracy.
- Give grace for varying levels of recall ability.

What are *Springboard* verses?

Springboard verses are marquis verses or pieces of verses that the student can learn easily. They usually characterize a particular concept or behavior very succinctly. If a student learns a verse quickly and easily, it builds confidence.

One springboard verse I always use is Galatians 1:9, "If any [man] preach any other gospel unto you than that ye have received, let him be accursed." It is easy to learn and reinforces the awareness that not all gospels are the same as the true gospel. As a side note, I almost always ask students to repeat 1 Corinthians 15:3-4 along with Galatians 1:9 to make sure they understand just what the Gospel is.

After the students have memorized a verse, what do I do next?

Once the students have memorized a verse, they need to be instructed as to what it means and what the ramifications are for their lives. People need to be taught. Memorization only gives oral learners the Word of God; it does not necessarily guarantee them understanding. "And Philip ran thither to [him], and heard him read the prophet Isaiah, and said, Understandest thou what thou readest? And he said, How can I, except some man should guide me? And he desired Philip that he would come up and sit with him" Acts 8:30-31.

How can I vary the repetition/correction exercises to make the learning process fun and interesting?

Since delivery must be done for student retention and repetition, it helps to mix up the repetition exercises. Here are some helpful methods.

- Use small segments and make sure the phrases are repeatable.
- Chop up the phrases.
- Use word substitution.
- Use phrase substitution.
- Use climactic memorization by adding a couple of words to each repeat cycle. For example, "For God so loved. For God so loved the world. For God so loved the world that He gave."
- A teacher can also, adjusting her volume, slow things way down or speed things up.
- Use a change of positions: standing, sitting, group recitation, or pairing.
- Change who repeats: women, men, front row, back row, etc.
- Add motions.
- Add inflection.
- Add rhythm.
- Add exaggeration.
- Use a vocal climax in volume.

- Intentionally use the opposite word needed.
- Intentionally leave out phrases or words.
- Employ reduplication—repeating a word in succession for emphasis.
- Use elimination—place several improper words in the right place until the person recognizes the correct word.
- Material incentives or rewards for learning—candy, stickers, etc.

Once a verse (or the verses) has been learned, what can the trainer do so that *students can teach* about meaning and ramifications?

It is a good idea to have oral discussion of the verses and their meanings. Since we are trying to reduce lecture time and encourage peer training, a significant amount of time should be spent requiring oral commentary between students. They should be talking in groups about the verses they have learned. Here are a few suggestions about group time.

- Ask students to explain what they think the verse means.
- Ask students to quote the verse with mistakes and have their partner correct their mistake.
- Ask students to talk about how living out the verse in their home might create conflict.
- Ask students to pray about the verse and how they can apply it today and tomorrow.
- Ask students to come up with a motion to accompany this verse.
- Ask students to interview each other by asking their own questions about the verse.
- Do group problem solving. Present a scenario involving the behavioral ramifications of living out the doctrine you teach and ask the students to solve a difficult problem.
- Restructure the small groups often to create variety and change.
- Create "good, better, best scenarios" for applying the verse.
- Have groups create 3 problem compromises with the doctrine or verse.

- Have a quotation time with a saboteur who corrects or wrongly corrects the person quoting; the saboteur must be corrected.
- Have them talk about a problem in the culture raised by the Bible verse.
- Have people do problem solving by asking pairs or groups to address how the church can come to doctrinal unity over the issue that is presented.

At subsequent lessons, what do I do?

If you have developed the lessons correctly, you will have an incremental BOP Ladder. Your lessons will build, and people will be excited about the learning process and method.

You must have a strict accountability practice at multiple levels. There should be a culture of expectation developing, not only with respect to the current lesson, but also with respect to the previous lesson. Since retention is a value, it is imperative that previous lessons be reinforced. The first part of every class should be taken up in repeating and reciting previous verses.

You must supervise the growing doctrinal superstructure. There will be local conflicts unique to your setting, perhaps with a church or a cult. There may be ideological battles that will brew as the Spirit of God takes control of the people in the group. Values clashes are inevitable. Because they must be treated with love, it is a good idea to have a verse early on in your memorization process that deals with the love of the church.

After the first lesson, what do I do?

After your first lesson, you must observe and modify the community-based model you have created. Collectively, the group will have immediately assimilated much of what you have taught them. However, you will have some changing to do. The model must be monitored, corrected, and multiplied. Once you have adapted the model and the repetition exercises to correctly fit your context, you will have a pedagogy that is right for your people group. You will have a contextually appropriate oral teaching model that is reproducible.

What does a sample lesson content look like?

It is a good idea to choose foundational verses that address seminal ideas. For example, consider the following:

1. John 3:3 Jesus answered and said unto him, Verily, verily, I say unto thee, Except a man be born again, he cannot see the kingdom of God.
2. John 14:6 Jesus saith unto him, I am the way, the truth, and the life: no man cometh unto the Father, but by me.
3. Luke 10:27 Thou shalt love the Lord thy God with all thy heart, and with all thy soul, and with all thy strength, and with all thy mind; and thy neighbor as thyself.
4. Acts 2:42 And they continued steadfastly in the apostles' doctrine and fellowship, and in breaking of bread, and in prayers.
5. 2 Timothy 2:2 And the things that thou hast heard of me among many witnesses, the same commit thou to faithful men, who shall be able to teach others also.

What does a more complete systematic theology look like?

It should resemble grounding aspects that are germane to every basic theology, but should also include culturally appropriate verses that focus on precise issues unique to your setting. In our setting, we have a laminated card from which we continually drill the twenty key verses we have isolated and that we feel will establish believers in the fundamentals of the faith.

Here is a list of basic theological verses that follow traditional systematic theology constructs. From this list you should be able to select a fair number of important doctrines around which you can build a BOP ladder. [5]

---

[5] Many of the ensuing Bible verses have been taken from "The Baptist Faith and Message," a doctrinal statement adopted by the Southern Baptist Convention on June 14th, 2000.

<u>What is the Bible all about?</u>
John 5:39
John 20:31

<u>Is man totally depraved and is God really angry about it?</u>
Romans 1:18
Romans 3:10
Romans 3:23

<u>What is Sin?</u>
1 John 3:4
James 4:17
Genesis 2:17
Romans 5:12
Galatians 3:10

<u>How am I saved from this sin and can I be saved by my good works?</u>
Ephesians 2:8-9
Titus 3:4-7

<u>Is Jesus the only way?</u>
John 14:6
Acts 4:12
1 Timothy 2:5

<u>What does it mean to be "in Christ?"</u>
Colossians 1:27-28
John 15:5

<u>How should I live my life?</u>
1 Corinthians 10:31.
Luke 10:25-28
Acts 1:8

<u>How serious should I be about my Christian faith?</u>
Acts 2:42
Jude 1:3-4
Galatians 1:8
2 Timothy 2:2
2 Corinthians 10:4-5
Philippians 2:12
2 Timothy 4:3
1 John 4:1

<u>How serious should leaders in the church be about being a thorough teacher of the gospel?</u>
Titus 1:9
Act 20:26-28

<u>Are the scriptures without error?</u>
2 Timothy 3:16-17
Hebrews 4:12-13
Matthew 5:18

<u>Where in the Bible does it tell me I should study the word of God regularly?</u>
2 Timothy 2:15
John 20:31

<u>What is the definition of the Gospel?</u>
1 Corinthians 15:1-3

Who is God and what are His qualities?
Psalm 90:2
Malachi 3:6
James 1:17
1 Kings 8:27
Jeremiah 23:24
Isaiah 40:22
Psalm 147:5
Romans 16:27
Genesis 17:1
Revelation 19:6
Isaiah 57:15
John 17:11
John 4:24
Revelation 4:8
Deuteronomy 32:4
Romans 2:4
Exodus 34:6
Psalm 117:2

What is the Godhead?
1 John 5:7
2 Corinthians 13:14.

Is a man justified by faith or accepted by God because he is a good person?
Galatians 2:16
Romans 1:16 – 17

Is God sovereign or is it all up to me?
John 15:16
Ephesians 1:11
Ephesians 1:4-7
Acts 13:48
Ephesians 2:10
Romans 9:22-23

Was Jesus really born of a virgin?
Isaiah 7:14

Is Jesus eternally God?
John 8:58
John 1:1-2
John 10:30
Rev 7:15-17

Where in the Bible does it talk about the resurrection and why is it important?
1 Corinthians 15:17
Colossians 3:1
1 Corinthians 15:21-22

Is there freedom in the Christian faith and if so, how much?
2 Corinthians 3:17
Galatians 2:4
Galatians 5:1
Galatians 5:13

Does each believer have the Holy Spirit?
Ephesians 4:30
Romans 8:9

Where does the Bible speak about the Second Coming of Christ?
Revelation 1:7
1 Thessalonians 4:16
Revelation 22:12
Isaiah 48:12

Does each person have to be baptized by immersion? Is baptism by sprinkling acceptable?

Matthew 28:18-20
Acts 8:38

Is the Lord's Supper (Communion) important?

1 Corinthians 11:23-27
Matthew 26:26-27
1 Corinthians 10:16

Does every Christian have a missionary responsibility?

Acts 1:8
Luke 10:5-6
Romans 10:14
Jude 1:23-24

When someone tells me I should worship on Saturday, what can I say?

Colossians 2:16
Romans 14:5
Romans 14:6

Do I have to live a holy life?

Galatians 2:20
1 Corinthians 6:19-20
Luke 9:23-24.
1 Corinthians 3:16-17

Vocalization Sixteen
The Oral Road Ahead

I want to present to you a few nuts and bolts that will help you see the need to develop advanced oral pedagogy habits. Many educated Christians have never been trained in oral communication and think they know how to teach to oral peoples simply because they know how to teach literates or preach behind a pulpit. This is not the case, however.

A great many complex oral instructional habits are essential in oral teaching settings. This is certainly the case in controlled attention environments among oral peoples. In these settings, all that exists is an oral learner with no books and no pencils. The teacher will be before a group that seems to be simply all eyes and ears. If you do not know what you are doing and have not practiced oral pedagogy, you will feel enormously self-conscious and might even fail at reaching the crowd.

It is my firm conviction that it will take you much longer to become an oral teacher if you exclusively do reading about oral learning. You may never become an oral teacher at all if all you do is read about orality.

You can start to learn to be an oral teacher in fifteen minutes by seeing and hearing someone practice carefully delivered narrative and who uses oral accountability and repetition. There is no substitute for hearing oral pedagogy.

Observational descriptions of orality can never replace oral modeling and apprenticeship. Missionaries cannot be expected to do what they have never seen. When we show video or PowerPoint projections to describe "orality," we contradict ourselves. Consequently, lectures on orality need to be replaced by practice sessions, visual demonstrations, and oral discipleship pedagogies.

The embodiment principle of oral cultures needs to replace our informational principle; otherwise we begin a fundamentally vocal apprenticeship with western-style lecture or reader-based methods.

Missionaries need to learn repetition drills, oral gesturing, story cycling, motif recognition, tonal importance, bodily reinforcement, syllabic grouping, feeling tone, and any of a number of fundamental elements of voice including, but not limited to, immediacy, volume, pitch, timbre, rhythm, register, pause, space, separation, repetition, range, intensity, speed, tension, intention, schematization, emotion, intensity, reception, embodied energy.

Missionaries working with oral peoples should also know how to do genre identification in order to be able to create culturally appropriate, brief, reproducible discipleship clips, namely: story, riddle, ballad, epic, proverb, motto, lament, recitation, chant, litanies, etc.

Missionaries need to know how to do listener aptitude diagnostics to be able to judge acquisition speed. This in turn becomes useful when creating common, auditory discipleship "systems." But be this as it may, it is impossible in a primer. We are stuck with the basics.

I want to say one final word about oral contextualization. Oral delivery is constantly contextualizing. It is not like print that never fits the context and never embodies theology. Consequently, it is imperative to master the skill of contextualization.

In order to do that, the missionary has to be adept at separating out the often subtle layering of culture. There are usually several important contexts that live in a situation at any given time. Some of these contexts may include the physical, verbal, religious, gender, sensorial, cultural, melodic, and gestural, just to name a few.

Each context brings with it oral rules. What is appropriate in one context may not work in another. Volume and tone in one, for example, may be disastrous in another. Local patterns and manners formalize delivery and dictate what kind of movements and gestures are typical.

Context may have ramifications for who can speak. It may be that there are age limitations in certain places or if the other sex is present. Each type of discourse may demand special conditions that are controlled by tradition.

Contextual conventions are sometimes unwritten. They must be learned, however, if the missionary is to be effective over the long term. When the missionary speaks, he must be speaking within the limits of cultural convention. Otherwise he is outside the contextual norm and his message is weakened.

There are always unwritten rules about distance and communication. How far away should someone be? How long can they talk?

The audience is also pre-programmed to some extent. Some may not be free to be genuine and at ease. Other settings require relaxed and informal learning situations.

Teachers are often stereotyped in a culture. They may be stereotyped by gender, by apprenticeship, by age, or by subject. It behooves the missionary to find the prescribed limits the culture has set for teachers, poets, prophets, religious men, etc.

How a culture allows a teacher to explain his information may have preset guidelines. An oral teacher may find an open door based on the prescribed format for oral delivery. As long as communication takes place within those prescribed limits and within *hear*-and-now, it is likely that the listeners will appreciate the attempt by the foreigner to accommodate himself to the setting.

It is my hope that no matter what your context, you lift Jesus up and give glory to God. He must increase but we must decrease. No oral context should be without a living Savior high and lifted up. However faulty your oral teaching may be, it is certainly filled with the Spirit of God if Jesus is in the middle of it. It never hurts to repeat what God never tires of hearing.

Parable Seventeen
The Parable of the Caterpillar People

Frank was a tropical Frog who was once a sinful tadpole before he was converted. He was a mature Frog preacher who spoke deep billowing tones that most of the other Frog people could not even attempt. He was considerably overweight from eating far too many flies at the lily pad suppers, but that was beside the point.

Frank had a burden for the Caterpillar people. Although he won many tadpoles to Frogdom, he knew that God wanted to make something wonderful of the Caterpillar people. He saw hidden beauty in all those ugly legs and strange furry hair.

The other Frog administrators stood against Frank when he stood up at a Frog business meeting and announced that he wanted to start a mission to the Caterpillar people. After all, they could not read, and reaching them meant putting aside the Gecko books wherein were written all the original teachings and truth of literate Frog people.

Frank stood his swamp ground and announced that he would use oral methods and stories to reach the Caterpillar people. Frank went to preach to the Caterpillar people, leaving behind his Gecko library. He gave it away to the young Frog students and Frog churches.

After many years, the Caterpillar people eventually learned to trust the big frog, believing he was not there to eat them for dinner. They took to heart his message to abide in the cocoon attached to the vine branch.

Many Caterpillar people began to emerge as beautiful blue butterflies. They filled the forest with beauty. Some were eaten by predators, but the forest was never the same again.

Frank was buried under a banyan tree with a little wooden cross. He died of a rare Frog virus. However, year after year, myriads of Butterflies would come and rest in the branches around Frank's grave and sing songs in Butterfly language.

Even the Frogs who never left the pond had to admit that Frank's oral methods worked. Some of them were so convinced of the fruitfulness that they themselves repeated Frank's system and mastered snake, lizard, and spider languages and learned to tell parables in many other uninscribed forest languages. The forest world became a beautiful place, all because Frank left his alphabet behind.

Post Word Review

.

It has been my goal in this short treatise, to introduce the reader to some of the basics of missionary orality issues and to advance missionary preaching and discipleship beyond the strictures of abstraction and heavy reading dependence.

Repetition, story, call and response, figured forms of proclamation, and simple phrase memorization are often the most appropriate means of evangelism and discipleship for house churches, cell groups, storying locations, and other pioneering locales.

Traditional Christian proclamation in literate settings has been built around a model that facilitates the speaker's management of material through theoretical categories and outlining methods. The practical outworking of that model demands abstraction, categorical classification, syllogistic logic, and extensive subordination.

Such methods of grouping material and systematizing thoughts do not always help hearers comprehend meaning because listeners do not simply construct sense through the clarification of conceptualized ideas. Many peoples of the world, including some in the so-called 'West', have storied ways of organizing thought. They also can only memorize small tidbits of information at one time.

Listeners often build sense by constructing analogies to life experience. This analogical process produces understanding and is sometimes aided by narrative sequence, but not always.

The use of organizational abstraction by missionaries, teachers, and preachers has put distance between the pulpit and pew, or if you are in the third world, between the speaker and the bench, or between the mound and the ground.

On the mission field, that distance is magnified enormously when the speaker, who is likely a semi-literate, attempts to employ non-native thought structures with an audience that is even less literate than he or she. If the leader also demands the memorization of long stories, he compounds the problem even further.

Much proclamation form that is currently employed in mission settings is learned with the aid of categorical thinking, the kind of abstraction one masters through the literacy process. European categories and views of texts have shackled up oral forms.

Unfortunately, we have done our fair share of exportation around the globe. Spontaneity, concreteness, beauty, and wonder are rare when abstraction prevails. More importantly, engagement is gone. Orality and its power disappear.

The emotional connection between speaker and listener is minimized under an abstracted teaching methodology because the speaker is overly concerned about extended storied sequence, expositional elements, and a cognitive transfer of information. The instinctual oral creation faculties are quelled to make room for prolonged ordered delivery.

Paradoxically, the day-to-day manner of communication among the more orally inclined people is abandoned in the context of the church. Church becomes formal. Sure, evangelical churches are Bible-based, text-centered. But the language and thought forms of literacy don't have to dictate communication choices and replace effective, hearer-based strategies that one finds in common life settings.

The missionary should repudiate much of his adopted highly discursive, instructional form, the one imported from his literate education. Most orally inclined people who are listening to the gospel for the first time prefer the use of Bible stories and images, short memorization chunks, verbally charged talk, and other narrative forms.

These culturally appropriate communication media just listed are usually native to oral contexts. They are found to be more effective in moving audiences and changing ideas. The task of emancipating missionaries from learned discursive delivery (that is, talk that is logical and literate), involves creating new ways of looking at communication.

We need to be honest enough to admit that Jesus used oral engagement method. We also need to be brave enough to practice the same model. Christ's principal engagement tool was the parable. At times, He used nothing else.

In order to accomplish the liberation of the highly educated missionary from his high-literate bondages, we need to begin to understand the nature of orality as participatory, embodying the change agent of gospel. When the missionary learns that spoken words show love and carry power, he or she is on the road to transforming ministry from a book-based, informational progression to a verbal, Spirit-filled interchange. He then will change the world, not through the power of oral rhetoric, however, but through the simple proclamation of the crucified and risen Christ, the Son of the Living God. Within that oral declaration, Jesus will indeed build his church, a church against which the gates of hell shall not prevail.